CONTENTS
WARBIRD JETS

5 **Beware Jet Blast!**
Paul Coggan looks at the warbird jet scene in the past, at present, and expresses his opinions on potential future developments.

7 **Last of the Lightning Pilots**
Ian Black, author of LIGHTNING outlines his experiences as the last RAF Pilot to go through the Lightning Training flight course at RAF Binbrook in this extensive, superbly illustrated Pilot Report exclusively for Warbirds Worldwide.

10 **Jet Heritage**
Adrian Gjertsen, formerly closely associated with the Hunter One Collection outlines some exciting new plans for a new venture: Jet Heritage – An exclusive first report.

12 **Sensational Sabre**
F–86 Sabre specialist Duncan Curtis takes an in depth look at the service history of the type and looks at potential areas for acquisition.

22 **Triumph and Tragedy**
A. Pascal Mahvi tells of his experience of flying the A–4 Skyhawk, how his close friend Raymond Guy Neeley was killed and the lessons to be learned from his tragic death. Photography by Thierry Thomassin.

28 **Flying the CAC Sabre**
Group Captain David Leach RAAF, details the first post-rebuild test flight of the RAAF's CAC built Sabre.

32 **Fouga Fever!**
The Fouga CM170 Magister is being imported to the U.S.A. in growing numbers and is proving to be a popular jet for many operators. J.C. Lutringer gives us a pilot report on one such aircraft, and the Editor looks at the source for the majority of the airframes.

35 **Dassault Mystere IV**
One type often overlooked on the warbird jet front is the *Ailes Francaises de la Chasse* Mystere IVA. Roland Fraissinet takes a brief look at the aircraft.

36 **MiG Alley Latest**
MiGs from various sources and of varying mark continue to flow into the United States. We look at the latest imports and activities at the two main MiG centres in the U.S.A., Reno, home of CIA Aviation, and Chino, home of Unlimited Aircraft Limited.

40 **GNATS!**
The Folland and Hindustan Aeronautics built Gnat is becoming popular as a warbird jet . . .

41 **Once Bitten . . .**
Texas based Charles parnall guides us through the rebuild of his ex RAAF T.Mk 35 Vampire

44 **MiG-21 Profile**
John Wilmslow profiles the infamous Fishbed; the latest MiG import to the United States.

Front Cover: *(RAAF Official) CAC Sabre A94–983 airborne during its first test flight in March 1986.* **Rear Cover: Top** *(Paul Coggan) The Combat Jet's Flying Museum's Canadair Sabre with its startling Korean Theatre warpaint at Oshkosh in 1988 and* **Lower** *(Bob DeGroat) Ex French air force '240' Fouga CM170 Magister is one of several such machines imported to the U.S.A. by Basler flight Services of Wisconsin.*

SAAB 32A Lansen N5468X alias Fv Nr 32209 painted n two tone matt grey with shocking pink and black titles – owned by Mac Two flight Services Inc. of California (Thierry Thomassin photo).

Beware: Jet Blast!

Undoubtedly the fastest moving aspect of warbirds today is jet operations. Whether the piston purists accept it or not warbird jets are here to stay. The upturn in activity, particularly in the last two years is largely due to the disposal of the earlier generation jet equipment. Worldwide, as you will see from reading the pages of this *Warbirds Worldwide Special Edition*, jet ops are thriving. As an introduction to this special I felt an overview of past and current happenings, with a few predictions for the future is a good idea. And the future has a lot to offer, with some exciting new types and projects in prospect.

As long as 1970, the Royal Australian Air Force released some 14 deHavilland Vampire T.35s. These were immediately exported to the United States where they have formed the backbone of the jet movement for some years, though types like the Lockheed and Canadair T-33s and a smaller number of North American F-86s where probably the first types to be operated as warbirds in the true sense many years earlier. Nevertheless, *Westair International* quickly passed on the majority of these airframes and more recently several have been changing hands and taking to the air in an increasing numbers. Similarly Australia have themselves a number of Vampires and the twin boom fighter is certainly popular there too. Latest news on the Vampire scene there is that Alan and Judy Pay have, with two other partners, imported seven Vampires from Zimbabwe, backed up with some twelve containers of spares.

Paul Coggan takes a brief look at the past, present and potential warbird movement across the world

The bulk of the airframes are FB.9 variants with two T.11 trainers. All are said to be flyable with minor items missing, though external refurbishment will be required. There are also some Vampires in the UK in the shape of the *Vintage Aircraft Team's* Vampire T.11 WZ507/G-VTII and, with the same organisation, T.11 XH328 which is also being rebuilt to fly.

As we said earlier the United States is the hub where warbirds are concerned and the jet population is growing apace. Jim Robinson's ambitious and acclaimed *Combat Jets Flying Museum* in Houston, Texas, is currently at the centre of a programme, with the full co-operation of the majority of jet operators, and the Federal Aviation Administration, to ensure the security of the jet ops there. The FAA are showing concern over the number of jet aircraft currently coming onto the register, and are taking a close interest in proceedings. The tame Vampires have been, in recent years, supplemented by ever more ferocious and powerful stablemates in the shape of Starfighters, A-4s, and a host of MiG variants, the latest of which is the MiG-21 – hence the profile on this aircraft elswhere in this publication. To put the United States in perspective as far as jets go there are currently some 28

Vampires and Venoms on the register in company with 92 Lockheed and Canadair T-33s, 23 Fouga CM170 Magisters, 31 Hispano Aviacion HA-200 and 220 Saeta's and dozens of various MiG variants from the MiG-15 through 17s, 19s and the latest 21s. The latter are mainly from Poland and China. The Fouga Magisters are dealt with elsewhere in this issue.

The Hispano Aviacion Saeta (Spanish for Arrow) is a popular aircraft introduced by Texas based Nathanuel Kalt, and Ray Stutsman's Indiana based Combat Aircraft.The Saeta is a tandem two- seat basic trainer. The HA-200A, B and D variants are powered by two Turbomeca Marbore II turbojets of 880lbst with the E variant having the more powerfull Marbore IV rated at 1058lbst. This little lightweight trainer, despite some early problems with documentation (all the manuals had to be translated from Spanish to English) has proven very popular in the U.S.A.

Other types gaining popularity are the Gnat – several of which have been sold by the U.K. based Ministry of Defence with a handful going to the United States and its Hindustan Aeronautics manufactured equivalent the Adjeet, several of which have turned up at Chino in California for rebuild, being ex Indian Air Force airframes.

The North American and Canadair variants of the F-86 and CL-13 Sabre have long been operated as warbirds, with several airframes being operated on government contract work by Tracor Flight Systems and Flight Systems

International. The Sabres are now, apparently being phased out, but this will not have any adverse affect on warbird jet operations. In Australia the Department of Administrative Services recently put a damaged Sabre – in the shape of A94-965 – up for tender in Sydney. The aircraft was sold for AUS$26,000 to Grif Air and is a likely candidate to fly. The DAS are apparently considering considering repeating the exercise with another aircraft. Additionally some more Commonwealth Aircraft Company Sabres will be up for sale shortly – see Warbirds Worldwide Number Seven for all a full report.

Almost certainly the most ambitious warbird jet project to date, certainly in the U.K. is the acquisition, by Arnold Glass, of six ex Royal Air Force Lightnings. Three two seat T.5s and three single seat F.6s were acquired by Arnie last June and were flown to Cranfield in Bedfordshire. It is understood that at least one T.5 and one F.6 will be maintained in an airworthy condition with the others being placed up for sale. These aircraft present a challenge to any jet operator, but taking into account that equally 'difficult' types are being operated in the United States then it is not an impossible task. As we go to press the Ministry of Defence are deciding the fate of an ex Aircraft and Armament Experimental Establishment Lightning T.5, XS422. This is basically the shell of a low houred airframe. Though large numbers

of both single and two seat Lightnings have been disposed of by the MoD most have had their wings torched just outboard of the main gear to allow transportation on a low-loader by road. Though '422 is just a shell it represents perhaps the last chance – outside of the Arnold Glass machines – for someone to acquire a Lightning for rebuilding to fly. One T.5, XS451, has apparently already left for the United States where it will be rebuilt for Flight Systems Inc., though it is unclear at this stage whether or not the aircraft will be flown as a warbird or on government contract. British Aerospace at Warton have been the custodians of some 22 ex Saudi Air Force Lightnings – 18 F.53s and 4 T.54s. As we go to press it is understood that 17 of these aircraft have been acquired by an English businessman along with a substantial spares holding, indicating that they are not going to the breakers yard. The remaining five aircraft are apparently being supplied to Museums, though again it seems likely that to be moved from Warton the wings will be torched, thus making them ground-bound forever. If these aircraft do go to the United States, and are for manned flights in government contract work, then it is possible that this would assist the operation of at least one or two as warbirds, though this would still be an expensive undertaking.

Poland and China have been the source for some very interesting jet warbirds

including MiG-15s, 17s, 19s and more recently MiG-21s. These machines are being flown regularly and operated as civil aircraft in a very professional way. The FAA have now allotted several LOA's (Letters of Authorisation) to pilots to fly the type, despite initial teething problems with paperwork and indoctrination training. There are now several MiG-21s in the United States and we can look forward to some very exciting displays and aircraft in the future.

And what for the future? It is my belief that what we have seen so far is just the tip of the iceberg. It must be remembered that there are a lot more jet aircraft of the same generation as the F-86, Hunter and MiG-15 to 21. We are already seeing F-104s and F-5s being rebuilt – and indeed flying. The French Air Force, as an example, are currently phasing out final numbers of Dassault Mirage IIIs – the first flight of this type took place on November 17th 1956, and there are many other jets of this era. Already we have seen SAAB Drakens and Lansens operating in the U.S.A., admittedly on a limited basis and mainly for contract work, but their operation by a civilian agency, in whatever role, has set the precedent for the future. By the end of the decade more elaborate and complicated jets will be flying as warbirds. Signs declaring BEWARE JET BLAST will soon be on many more warbird flight lines across the world! **WW**

Paul Coggan

Lightning T.5 serial XS422 last flew from Boscombe Down in September 1987. With just over 2000 hours on the airframe it is now a shell, and is up for tender by the UK Ministry of Defence as we go to press. It represents, outside of the six machines owned by Arnold Glass and the ex Saudi machines, the last chance to preserve a Lightning in flying condition. The chances are it will go to the breakers, or at best to a museum. (**Crown Copyright – A&AEE Boscombe Down**).

Last of the Lightning Pilots

Three years ago the choices for a trainee pilot, having completed the Attack and Weapons training course on Hawks at RAF Brawdy and having been assessed for suitability for a high workload environment, (possibly single-seat) were either single seat Air Defence or F–4 Phantom, or in the ground attack role; Tornado, Buccaneer (Maritime), Harrier or Jaguar. Each aircraft had its benefits but for me there was only one choice. The Lightning, possibly the meanest aircraft ever to leave a British factory.

Having grown up around the Lightning it was a dream of mine to fly in an aircraft but only a fantasy to pilot one. Everything about the Lightning captured me – I had to fly it. Posting time came and it was with more than a little trepidation that I downed my pint pot, to read the word *Lightning* stuck to the bottom! The dream had started. Attending the mandatory pre-OCU (Operational Conversion Unit) courses my compatriot and I were told how very lucky we were to be on the last LTF Course (Lightning Training Flight) and how many had passed before use.

Driving up the hill to RAF Binbrook brought back many childhood memories – the snow, howling gales and frequent rain, not to mention fog. Soon it was to become a way of life again. As a boy I used to gaze at the runway with my elder brother, watching 5 Squadron aircraft take-off and landing and rushing off to intercept the resident Canberra and Meteor aircraft of 85 Squadron. How odd it was to be back, twenty years later, standing amongst enthusiasts and knowing that soon I would be on the other side of the fence getting to grips with the *Ferrari* of fighter aircraft.

Flight Lieutenant **Ian Black,** the last Royal Air Force pilot to pass through the Lightning Training course at Binbrook tells the story of his transition onto type and his experience flying the finest single seat jet ever produced in the UK.

If you ever went into the LTF crewroom at Binbrook you will have surely seen one of the most incredible pieces of post-war wall art of an early flying machine covering an entire wall complete with all the Lightning foibles and faults; a fascinating painting. You could only feel more than a little humble entering the coffee bar, thinking you were once king of the skies having completed the Hawk weapons course at Brawdy, to be surrounded by seven or eight Lightning instructors all wearing 1000 hour badges many of them who were Intercept Weapons Instructors, Qualified Flying Instructors or merely Tactics Instructors.

The flying side of the Royal Air Force is one of lifes great levellers. Coffee over, it was time to go outside for a course photograph in front of the LTF Flagship, a high fatigue Mk. 6 aircraft with a fuel pack fitted instead of the usual guns, to give it an increased endurance as an airborne target for the units T.5 and F.3 aircraft. After a very civilised weeks ground school it was into the simulator for a further weeks emergency training. Luckily the use of the four inch torture tube (in the right hand corner, called the radar) was to come later. At the end of a weeks basic simulator flying it gave me a fair idea that the next six months was not going to be easy. Ground school over it was up to the LTF to begin the CONVEX

(Conversion Exercises) phase. This normally comprised of five dual sorties, then a solo sortie, then a mixture of random dual and solo sorties alternating in the T.5 and F.3. The T.5 had an awkward cockpit both in terms of size and instrumentation layout, with all the main flight instruments grouped in the centre of the cockpit. This gave an instant parallax problem with the side-by-side seating. The first impression of the T.5, and somewhat off-putting was its enormous size, like a giant feline beast waiting to pounce. This aircraft was a good deal bigger than the tiny Hawk I'd been used to some two weeks previously.

The cockpit was some ten feet off the ground and access could only be gained by using the awkward ladder strung underneath the in-flight-refuelling probe. You had to be a small contortionist to climb the ladder, in full flying kit, whilst going under and over the probe to gain access to the cockpit. At first, strapping in was also laborious, coming from the Hawk which had a simple lap and shoulder restraint system; the Lightning had a far more complex and ancient system of straps, buckles and quick-release boxes. Prior to each sortie the engineering F700 (form 700) was always checked in the engineering line hut. The '700 was basically like a car service schedule showing any minor faults or major faults which required rectification on the aircraft. Arriving at the Lightning the customary pilot 'walk-round' would be carried out before each sortie. Starting on the left hand side with the nose wheel-well a quick check of the nose-wheel doors to ensure they would move freely, and onto the radome area. A cursory check of the radome to ensure that the bullet wasn't burnt and that

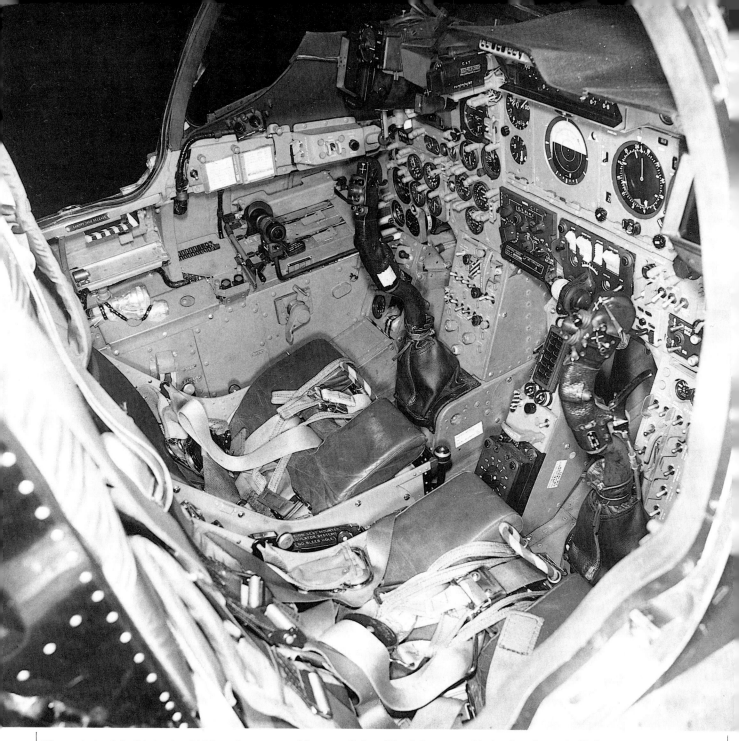

The cockpit of the Lightning T.5 is rather cramped but very fighter like. It is unusual in having the main flight instruments grouped in the centre of the cockpit – giving rise to an instant parallax problem. (**British Aerospace Warton**).

nobody had thrown any objects down the intake which would cause foreign object damage. Around to the right-hand side of the fuselage and it was time to check for any fuel leaks. The Lightning often leaked like sieves but as long as they leaked in the right place you were normally happy to take them. A good idea now to check the tyres, especially on a windy day, when tyres could get burnt out in one sortie. So well worn tyres were not normally accepted. Around the back of the aircraft and a check of the accumulator pressure gauges and a quick look down the jet pipe to look for any molten metal – a sure sign of turbine blade failure. A similar glance across the left hand side of the aircraft and it was time to climb the ladder and get strapped in.

Having strapped in and turned the main aircraft battery ON you could adjust the ejector seat height. This would also give you an indication of whether the voltage on the battery was good. Time to give the ground crew the signal to connect external power using AC and DC voltage. A quick look around the cockpit from left to right to ensure that nothing is missing and back to the throttle box to check full and free movement. As part of the engine start it was now vital to signal to the groundcrew that you wished to start the No. 1 engine. At engine start hot exhaust gasses are expelled from underneath the aircraft and anyone standing nearby could be badly burned. He returns your 'wind-up' signal, you open the throttle allowing the HP cock to open. Pulling the rapid start gang bar up with the LP cocks ON and selecting the start ice light switch to START you press the Start button for two seconds. Instantly a loud hissing explosion occurs behind you as half a gallon of AVPIN

(isopyl nitrate) ignites inside its combustion chamber, turning the Avon engine into life. A careful watch of the RPM gauge and the temperature gauge shows you how the start is going. On a hot day with a tail wind the engine will reach 800° Centigrade in two or three seconds. With number one engine running you can either use external power or disconnect it and bring the aircraft's own power on line to start number two engine. Quite often the aircraft will be temperamental during start, particularly in the rain or damp. On winter days at Binbrook it wasn't uncommon to see three or four ground crew climbing onto the spine of Lightnings hitting them furiously with a hammer in an effort to help it start!

With both engines running, relatively few checks were required prior to taxi. Checking that the ejector seat pins were out and your elbows were in it was time to close the canopy. Any previous thoughts you had about the cramped cockpit were now confirmed. Once the hood was down you felt like a mouse in a cage, surrounded by ironwork and with small windows to view through. A final check of the brake pressure and a quick flick of the taxi light on to show you were ready to move; parking brake OFF and she quickly pounces forward. Squeeze the brake and the tub nods down showing that both brakes are working well. A small kick of the right foot and a small squeeze on the stick mounted brake handle and the aircraft turns right with plenty of excess power to taxi even at idle thrust. Taxiing a large aircraft like the Lightning using the stick mounted brake lever and differential brakes was a bit tricky at first but became natural with time. Keeping the head moving whilst taxiing out to avoid hitting other aircraft you run through the pre take-off checks, basically to ensure you are going to get the aircraft airborne safely. If all else failed, four major checks could often save the day. CONTROLS that they were full and free, CAPTIONS that they were all out, PINS that you had four stowed and the seat was stowed and the seat was live and the CANOPY was down and LOCKED.

Lining up on the centre of the runway is not as easy at it looks. With those ultra-thin high pressure tyres the Lightning would skid and slide very easily on wet concrete, especially on the painted 'piano keys'. With clearance to take off and a final check of controls canopy and captions you apply the brakes and advance the throttles to FULL, checking that the RPM and the JPT (Jet Pipe Temperature) rise in the correct sense. With brakes holding at 92% a quick check around the cockpit to ensure everything is in order you release the brakes and slam the throttles forward. RPM up to 104%, JPT below 795° C, and checking the nozzle position. Already you have reached 100 knots by the RHAG (Rotary Hydraulic Arrester Gear) cable, checking the main standby airspeed indicator agree you soon find you are at 135 knots. Stick back and the nose wheel comes off, taking care not to scrape the tail as you do this. 155 knots and a small rearward check on the stick gets you airborne. Even with the enormous thrust available on the T.5 the aircraft still felt heavy with a cold-power take-off. A burner take-off in a T.5 is another story. Airborne with a positive rate of climb, the undercarriage is selected UP, checking the lights went from three greens to three reds and then out. This told you that the doors were clear and locked. On your first sortie at this stage your brain is still telling you you are still in the crew room, as she has already accelerated up to 450 knots, the Lightning climb speed. You instantly realise that with the nose about 10 to 15° above the horizon even in cold power that the aircraft is motoring. The standard climb out for Binbrook on runway 21 was a left hand turn onto a heading of 040° through the Blueway (airway Blue One) up to the normal level of FL250 (25,000 feet). You would normally be at this level by Spurn Point, just 15 miles North East of the airfield. Once you realise where you are it is time to level off. The first thing you need to do is take a fuel check. Already the small underbelly tank is almost empty, leaving only wing and flap fuel to complete the sortie. On this initial sortie just a few turns are performed to see how the Lightning handles, how much buffet is used and how docile the aircraft is at low speeds.

Now it is time to run through a simulated down-wind circuit leg at height, to give you an idea of what was to come. Speed reducing at back below 250 knots, undercarriage coming down, fuel sufficient for recovery, flaps travelling, harness tight and locked, checking you have three greens and that the toggle was engaged ie that the undercarriage was locked down. Tipping into a final turn at approximately 200 knots, on an imaginary runway the Lightning required a bit of pull and a bit of rudder to get it going around the corner. Heads back in again now and on to instruments, for an IF type turn. Holding at 190 knots, easy with the excess power and looking to roll out on finals with 175 to 170 knots. Watching your aiming point and holding the threshold in the middle of the windscreen. Popping the airbrakes out – to allow you to have a higher power setting than required – so that if you had to abort or land short a quick blip on the airbrakes which would retract them would give you extrainstant thrust. Still holding your imaginary runway on the nose and then watching the speed as the height reduces quickly, small adjustments in the power peg the speed at 170 knots and you cross the threshold, looking for 165 knots on touchdown. Climbing away, putting the gear and flaps up and popping the airbrakes in it is time to recover now for a PAR (Precision Approach Radar). This

Continued on Page 19

Now it is time to run through a simulated down-wind circuit leg at height . . .
(Ian Black).

Jet Heritage

The finest collection of flying historic British jets is reborn.

Jet Heritage's Operations Director **Adrian Gjertsen** outlines the plans for this exciting new collection.

The future of what is undoubtedly one of the World's finest jet aircraft collections now seems secure. Fortunately this unique fleet of jets will remain in Britain after more than two years of uncertainty since the untimely death of the previous owner, Michael Carlton. This has been made possible by rescuing the majority of the *Hunter One Collection* of restored early British jet aircraft from an uncertain fate and placing it with the newly formed *Jet Heritage Collection*. The new collection comprises the complete original *Hunter One Collection* (less the single seat Hunter G-HUNT, lost to Jim Robinson's *Combat*

selves the proud owners of two Jet Provosts, G-PROV and G-JETP.

The concept of re-establishing such a unique flying museum of jet aircraft was put to them by Adrian Gjertsen, formerly the operations director and manager of the *Hunter One Collection*, who had himself acquired Sea Hawk G-SEAH at the same auction. Ian and Dougal, who already had a deHavilland Vampire under restoration, and now two Jet Provosts, were taken with the idea and *Jet Heritage* was born with the subsequent addition of Hunter G-BOOM and Meteor G-LOSM. With the former *Hunter One Collection* as its starting point *Jet Heritage* will be dedicated to preserving the fine tradition of British jet aircraft and will secure a part of Britain's aviation heritage which would otherwise have become lost forever.

also progress into high performance jet aircraft and systems development; work has already commenced on a second Hunter T.7. The high standards of professionalism that were the hallmark of *Hunter One* will be maintained and enhanced under the leadership of Messrs. Gjertsen and Hayward. *Jet Heritage* will continue to restore and operate British jet aircraft, with the next long term restoration project soon to get under way – the rebuild of a Supermarine Swift which will be the only one of its type in the world to fly.

Jet Heritage intends to make its growing fleet of aircraft available for airshow appearances and film work with the possible future opening of an area for the public to see the restoration of the aircraft first hand. *Warbirds Worldwide* will be following the progress of the various projects and will be covering the new collection in greater detail in a future issue.

Painted bright red Hunting Jet Provost T.52A (equivalent to an RAF T.4) is an ex Singapore and South Yemen airframe registered in the UK in December 1983. Its overall black stable-mate, G–JETP ex XP666 has a similar background (**Arthur Gibson photo**).

Jets Flying Museum) plus some exciting new additions.

Following the death of businessman Michael Carlton in 1986 the future of this unique collection – a two seat Hawker Hunter, two Jet Provosts, a Gloster Meteor and a Hawker Sea Hawk, looked very unsure. After 18 months of uncertainty the collection came up for auction. Two longstanding aviation enthusiasts, brothers Ian and Dougal Craig-Wood, attended the auction and after some brisk bidding found them-

Jet Heritage will be based at a new hanger complex at Bournemouth Hurn airport, and the vast task of engineering maintenance and restoration will be headed up by none other than Eric Hayward, previously Chief Engineer with *Hunter One* and in whose hands the aircraft were lovingly restored. It is the intention to attract other historic jet aircraft to the site for hangarage, maintenance and restoration. Philip Meeson's deHavilland Venom is already based with *Jet Heritage*, and the business will

Colour captions opposite: *Top depicts Meteor NF.11 WM167 (registration G–LOSM) is painted in 141 Squadron, RAF colours and Lower Hawker Hunter T.7 G–BOOM, an ex Royal Netherlands and Royal Danish Air Force machine* (**Arthur Gibson**)

Operations will be managed by Adrian Gjertsen. Adrian can be contacted for airshow bookings and enquiries on 01-874-1572 (Telex: 94011109, Fax 01-871-9884).

The Sensational Sabre

Poetry in motion. Royal Canadian Air Force Sabre 19183. (**Military Aircraft Photographs**).

The title *classic jet* is frequently used nowadays, often in relation to aircraft of dubious heritage. However, one jet which can rightly claim to be a classic is the F–86 Sabre. Already gaining popularity with the warbird jet movement, the Sabre, in its various forms, still exists in fair numbers all over the world. Having seen combat from Taiwan to Argentina and from Pakistan to Korea, the Sabre has been exceeded in its widespread use only by the T–33, the Havard/Texan and the Dakota. In all thirty-nine nations have operated the type and this is the key to its widespread availability to potential warbird owners today.

The very first Sabre, North American XP–86 serial number 559597 was completed on 8th August 1947, and took to the air for the first time on the 1st October the same year with George Welch at the controls. This was the precursor of a production total of some 6317 built by North American at Los Angeles, California and Columbus, Ohio. This total includes 1149 of the *Fury* Naval derivative. Several countries also produced the Sabre under licence, namely the Commonwealth Aircraft Company in Australia (112 Rolls-Royce Avon powered CA–27s), Canadair in Canada (1814 Orenda powered CL–13s), Fiat in Italy (221 F–86Ks) and Mitsubishi in Japan (365 F–86Fs). Thus, in total, just under 10,000 were built. Within three years of its first flight the Sabre was given a chance to prove itself. On 25th June 1950 war broke out in Korea. F–86As from the Fourth Fighter Group

Warbirds Worldwide F–86 Specialist **Duncan Curtis** takes an in depth look at the classic Sabre with a look at its military service record, and details of where the type can still be found today.

were amongst the first to see action, Lt. Col. Bruce Hinton becoming the first jet pilot to shoot down another jet in combat in Korea when he downed a MiG–15 on 17th December 1950. At the end of hostilities 792 enemy aircraft had been shot down by Sabres in Korea; some 78 F–86s had been lost. This combat record enabled the Sabre to rate so highly with the world's air arms when the time came for jet procurement. The following gives an idea of where these aircraft went . . . and where to find them now.

Argentina received 28 F–86F–30s in 1960 after an initial deal for Canadair Sabres did not materialise. The *Fuerza Aerea Argentina (FAA)* Sabres were to dash 40 standard with longer wings and leading edge slats. These aircraft operated from El Plumerillo, where they formed three squadrons of the *Group 1 de Caza Bombardeo*. *FAA* Sabres saw action in April 1962 when they destroyed a Douglas C–54 on the ground in the course of putting down an attempted coup at Punta Indio. By 1976, 12 aircraft of the initial batch were left in service. Withdrawn from use and placed in storage, these aircraft were being prepared for export to Uraguay when the Falklands

war broke out. Although not directly involved in the aerial conflict the F–86s were pressed back into service to reinforce front line aircraft. The stay of execution was short lived. On 19th June 1986 aircraft serial C–120 suffered a fatigue-related wing separation over Rivadavia, and the Sabres service with the *FAA* was drawn to a swift conclusion. The remaining aircraft were withdrawn from service officially in July 1986, one aircraft (C–123) was donated to the USAF Academy at Colorado Springs and more recently two were exported to the United States by Rick Sharpe (111 and 119). Five or so remain in Argentina.

Australia took up production of the Sabre at the Commonwealth Aircraft Company, Fisherman's Bend near Melbourne. These aircraft, though utilising American parts, were, in reality, redesigned to accommodate the Rolls-Royce Avon 26 engine in place of the General Electric J–47. In order to complete this alternative powerplant the rear fuselage of the CA–27 had to be extensively modified. The CAC Sabre entered service with the Royal Australian Air Force in March 1956. Operating from Butterworth in Malaysia, CA–27s from No. 3 Squadron RAAF saw action against Malaysian terrorists in 1958. The last 69 aircraft built were equipped with fuel tanks in the wing leading edge. These Mk. 32 aircraft thus possessed a genuine 1500 mile range on full tanks. CAC Sabres eventually equipped four squadrons and an Operational Training Unit (OTU), the final aircraft in service being retired as late as 31st July 1971.

Currently over 20 remain in Australia, including eight at Wagga Wagga Air Force Base. *The RAAF Historic Flight* also maintain one in airworthy condition (see article elsewhere in this publication).

The **Bangladesh Air Force** used a limited number of abandoned ex Pakistan Air Force Canadair Sabres from 1971 onwards. Four of these aircraft were still in service in the mid 1970s, but were soon replaced by MiG–21MFs, and it is doubtful if any Sabres still survive in this part of the world.

The **Forces Aerienne Belge** saw limited use of the type (five F–86F–25s) when aircraft were delivered to Belgium in June 1955. Little is known of these aircraft but it can be assumed that they were for evaluation only; the Belgian Air Force later re-equipped with the Hawker Hunter and Republic Thunderstreak. One of the five aircraft was later delivered to the Republic of Korea Air Force.

One of the few air arms still operating the F–86 today is the **Fuerza Aerea Boliviana (FAB)**. Lack of funds lead to the FAB purchasing some nine ex Venezuelan Air Force F–86F–30s, brought up to dash 40 standard in 1973. These aircraft replace F–51D Mustangs, several of which ended up in Canada. The Sabres of the FAB have been operated by the *Grupo Aereo De Caza 32* at Santa Cruz throughout their career. Initially operating in a natural metal finish, FAB Sabres have since been overhauled at Cordoba in Argentina, and have received the FAA style three tone camouflage. A number of these aircraft have been lost in accidents, and two Sabres were seriously damaged on 11th July 1984 when a civilian Cessna crashed into the FAB

hangar at Santa Cruz. However, at least four aircraft are still serving with the FAB and following frustrated deals for F–104 Starfighters and Mirages (due to lack of finance) it would seem the only course of action is the purchase of further Sabres.

The **Burmese Air Force (Tamdaw Lay)** operated 12 Canadair Sabres from the mid 1970's, probably ex Pakistan Air Force. Lack of spares and funds precluded a long service life, and by the 1980s the Tamdaw Lay had lost most of its fighter capability.

The first country to take out a licence to build the Sabre was **Canada**, who built around 20% of the world's Sabres. As well as being exported the Canadair machines (built at Cartierville near Montreal) served with the Royal Canadian Air Force (RCAF) in large numbers from 1951. By the time of their official retirement in 1968 Sabres had served with thirteen front line Squadrons in the RCAF plus six auxiliary units. Canada is still a rich source of Sabre spares though demand is still great. Many operators consider the Canadair machine as the best of the line. *Flight Systems Inc.*, of Mojave, California, have been a large user of the CL–13 since its withdrawal from active service. However, over 20 Sabres remain in Canada, and two or three still serve with the RCAF though only as instructional airframes.

Canada exported several CL–13s to a number of countries including **Colombia**. In a deal which cost the *Fuerza Aerea Columbiana (FAC)* only $3 million, Canadair supplied six brand new Sabres 6s. These aircraft were accepted in May 1956 and formed *1 Escuadron de Caza Bombardiero* at German Olano air base. Replacing F–47D Thunderbolts in the

fighter bomber role, a number of F–86Fs supplemented the Canadian built machines from 1963. By this time only 3 CL–13s remained in service. In 1972 Dassault Mirage Vs finally replaced any survivors and another chapter of Sabre history was closed.

Undoubtedly the largest potential source of Sabre airframes in Europe these days is **Denmark**. Acquiring sixty F–86Ds in 1958, the Royal Danish Air Force (RDAF) equipped three squadrons, modified to accept Martin Baker ejection seats. RDAF Sabres passed from service in March 1966 giving way to the CF–104G Starfighter. More importantly though, apart from three aircraft which serve as gate guards, over 30 F–86Ds still serve as decoys at various RDAF air bases. Amongst these are 13 at Karup, 7 at Vandel, and 5 at Skydstrup. No doubt these aircraft will soon outlive their present use, and may become available for tender and sale to potential warbird operators.

Further afield, and often overlooked in air force surveys, the **Ethiopian Air Force (EAF)** have seen over 25 years service from the F–86. Delivered in 1960, 25 F–86F–30s were later reinforced by further deliveries from Iran in 1970, amongst which was at least one CL–13. By 1977, 12 Sabres were still flying from Debre Zebit, and these aircraft were active during the war with Somalia in 1978–79. Eritrean guerilla activity followed on from this conflict, and the destruction of 28 mainly Soviet-supplied aircraft at Asmara in May 1984 helped

A number of aerobatic teams have utilised the Sabre over the years. This aircraft belongs to the Royal Canadian Air Force's Golden Hawks **(Military aircraft Photographs)**.

The Sensational Sabre

extend the service life here of the Sabre.

Initially supplied in natural metal finish, the EAF later applied a three tone sand-green-brown camouflage scheme with light grey undersides. The F–86 was still serving with the EAF as late as February 1986 and due to their being overlooked for so long it is possible that these aircraft are still flying.

Surprisingly only one F–86K survives in **France** at the Musee de l'Air in Paris. Although the French Air Force/Armee de l'air operated 60 Fiat built F–86Ks from 1956 until 1962 all except one was returned to Italy or scrapped.

The same cannot be said of **Greece** where *Elliniki Aeroporia* operated some 104 CL-13s from 1955 and 50 ex USAF F–86Ds from 1960. The F–86Ds were mainly ex USAFE examples, overhauled by Fiat before delivery. By 1966 all five

1987 and are still in Honduras. All of these aircraft saw service with the Royal Air Force in the 1950s and it would be nice to see them flying again.

Meanwhile, not to be outdone by Canadair, CAC had started to export the CA–27, though not until it had almost passed out of RAAF service. **Indonesia** received sixteen ex RAAF CA–27 Mk 32s, in February 1976. These aircraft flew from Madium in Eastern Java and were still based there in the early 1980s. Recent deliveries of Northrop F–5s and General Dynamics F–16s must put their continued existence in doubt, though at least three are now preserved in the country and another three are with the Nurtanio aircraft factory at Bandung.

The **Imperial Iranian Air Force (IIAF)** was probably the briefest of Canadair Sabre users, serving as a go-between

in the reputed illegal sale of 90 ex *Luftwaffe* aircraft in 1966. Painted in *Luftwaffe* colours with IIAF roundels applied on top these aircraft went to Pakistan, ostensibly for overhaul but never to return. The IIAF did however operate a number of F–86Fs until the early 1970s and even founded an aerobatic team, the *Golden Crown* before turning to the Northrop F–5. Whether Sabres still exist in Iran may never be known as little information is forthcoming due to the current political situation.

Iran's neighbour **Iraq** also operated F–86Fs in limited quantities. Five were handed over in 1958 as the initial step in Iraqs re-armament. Unfortunately the overthrow of King Faisal II in July 1958 led to the follow-on delivery being vetoed by the U.S. Government.

1956 saw **Italy** taking delivery of 180

Japanese aerobatic team Blue Impulse *F–86F in 1973* (**MAP**).

squadrons of Sabres had been replaced by Northrop F–5s and F–104 Starfighters. A large number were then used as decoys, painted in sand and spinach camouflage and several still exist, notably at Alexis and Previza air bases, the predominant type being the F–86D.

Probably the last time the Sabre was rattled in anger was with the **Honduran** *Fuerza Aerea Hondurena (FAH)* in the early to mid 1980's against Nicaraguan forces on its western borders. The *FAH* operated some 4 ex Venezuelan F–86Ks, 9 Canadair CL–13s and an F–86F. The F–86Ks, supplied in 1969, saw limited service and were withdrawn by 1980. The CL–13s however, purchased from the Yugoslavian Air Force in the mid 1970s, were operated by *Escuadron Sabre* at San Pedro Sula until 1986. The aircraft were replaced by Dassault Super Mysteres in

This immaculate Japanese F–86F serial 72–7744 shows the classic lines (**Bill Fisher File**).

Canadair Sabres from the Royal Air Force. The Italian Air Force – *Aeronautica Militaire Italiana (AMI)* equipped 7 *Gruppi* with the CL–13 until the type was replaced by the F–86K and Fiat G–91 in 1960. Five AMI CL–13s were sent to the Congo in 1962 as part of a United Nations peacekeeping force. True to the international nature of the operation these aircraft were flown by Philippine Air Force pilots. One of these aircraft found its way to Kinshasa University in Zaire and can still be seen there. This aircraft, serial 19542 served in the RAF as XB639 with 67 Squadron in West Germany.

Twelve or more CL–13s still remain in Italy though they passed from active inventory more than 25 years ago. The F–86K assembled by Fiat, in many cases replaced the CL–13s from 1956. Sixty-five entered service and served the AMI until March 1973 when the last example was retired at Rimini. Many live on, amongst them four F–86Ks which arrived at a scrap yard at Castrette in 1987, one since moving to Padora another to Treviso and was pictured as such in *Warbirds Worldwide Number 5*. Another five F–86Ks were reported at Istrana in 1982 but have not been noted recently.

Japan still has a fair population of Sabres although their accessibility to potential owners may be in question. The *Japanese Air Self Defence Force (JASDF)* deployed a total of 435 F–86Fs and 122 F–86Ds making this country the third largest user of the type. Initial F–86Fs were purchased in 1955, 135 being delivered from the United States. Mitsubishi began assembling aicraft from U.S. shipped components and 300 were manufactured from 1957–61. When sufficient aircraft had rolled off the production line some 45 of the initial U.S. supplied batch were returned there. In 1959 the *JASDF* gained all-weather fighter capability with the delivery of 122 F–86Ds. Operations went relatively smoothly until 30th July 1971 when an F–86F, serial 92–7932 collided with a civilian Boeing 727 near Morioko. This accident resulted in the grounding of all *JASDF* aircraft for two months. Returning to service, the Sabres of *JASDF* continued until 8th February 1981 when the aerobatic team

Blue Impulse performed their last display at Iruma near Tokyo. The aircraft that remain in Japan (approximately 92 at the last count including 58 F–86Ds) face an uncertain future. Bought through the U.S. Military Assistance Programme these aircraft should either be scrapped or returned to the United States if the terms are to be met. Over 100 have already returned there for use as target drones by facilities at China Lake and Point Mugu. Of the Sabres still in Japan many are displayed at airports and military bases. Hopefully some may become available to far sighted warbird operators. On the other side of the world **Yugoslavia's** *Jugoslavensko Ratno Vazduhplovstvo (JRV)* has seen much service from their CL–13 Mk 4s and F–86Ds. Operating mainly from Batajnacica near Belgrade, 180 ex RAF CL–13s and 130 ex USAF F–86Ds were supplied from 1956–1961. the Canadair Sabres were replaced by Soviet equipment in the mid-1970s though the 'Ds soldiered on into the 1980s when some twenty, based at Skopje were replaced by MiG–21s. Recognising the contribution made to its country the Yugoslavs preserved examples of the F–86D at both Lubljana and Zagreb airports and no doubt several others are still extant. At least one ex *JRV* Sabre has found its way to the United States; 14024 was seen at Pasadena, Texas in 1987. Other aircraft could follow.

Presenting a better chance of viewing or acquisition are the remaining Sabres of the **Republic of Korea Air Force** *(ROKAF)*. Of the 122 F–86Fs and 40 F–86Ds supplied from 1956–58, some 50 were still in service as late as 1979 though it was around this period that the D models were withdrawn. The general aviation press continue to ignore *ROKAF* Sabre operations, often stating that F–5s had totally replaced the type, when F–86Fs could still be seen operating from Taegu in 1987. Some ex *ROKAF* Sabres have recently been received by the U.S. Naval Weapons Center at China Lake to serve the same purpose as their *JASDF* brethren and an F–86F has found its way into the hands of the Oregon Military Museum at Clakamas (serial 24755). Two F–86Fs and two F–86Ds are curren-

This Danish air force F–86D is used as a decoy and looks in a very poor state: Skydstrup 1977 (**Military Aircraft Photographs**).

tly preserved in South Korea.

First export customer for the Commonwealth Aircraft Company Sabre was **Malaysia,** which received some sixteen CA–27s from the RAAF between 1969 and 1971. These aircraft served at the former RAAF base at Butterworth where Sabre FM1905 is currently guarding the gate. Equipping Nos. 11 and 12 Squadron *Royal Malaysian Air Force* the F–86s were replaced by F–5s in 1976. In total four CA–27s withstood the ravages of time and preserved in museums or as gate guards.

The ubiquitous F–86K equipped three squadrons of the **Royal Netherlands Air Force**, the *Koninklijke Luchtmacht* from 1955 to 1964. Following service most of these aircraft were scrapped; one aircraft was placed atop a pylon at Twenthe Air Force Base. Ironically, when the Military Museum at Soesterburg required an F–86K for preservation they had to go to Italy. On 12th June 1973 aircraft 53–8305 ex AMI arrived at Deelen air base – it has since been painted in *KLU* colours as 'Q305' and is displayed alongside an ex Portugese Air Force F–86F restored in 32 FIS colours. The **Royal Norwegian Air Force** operated some 115 F–86Fs and F–86Ks from September 1955 to January 1968 serving seven squadrons. Wing centre section cracks on the *FNoAF* led to their retirement in 1966 after a period of restricted flying. The majority of the F–86Fs returned to the U.S.A. though two were diverted to Portugal for spares use, and a further three to Saudi Arabia. The F–86K fleet was withdrawn from use in 1967/8 and seeing no further use for them they were scrapped in Norway. Today, the *RNoAF* Museum possesses four F–86Fs and six F–86Ks, most of which are stored at Gardermoen, presumably as a pool for exchange for other aircraft on the museum's shopping list. One of the F's is now immaculately restored in 338 Squadron colours.

The Sensational Sabre

Many Sabre airframes still serve as decoys and **Pakistan** retains many for this purpose. Operating F–86Fs and CL–13s from 1956 and 1966 respectively, 210 in total were active with this air arm until phased out in the late 1970's and early 1980's *PAF* Sabres served in both the '65 and '71 conflicts with India and their exploits have been well covered in subsequent publications. Though operating against the agile Adjeet (Gnat) and Hunter the *PAF* Sabres, fitted with Aim–9 Sidewinder missiles still maintained a 5.6:1 kill ratio in their favour. Approximately 30 *PAF* Sabres still survive, decoys being located at Masroor AFB, including CL–13 c/n 1815, the last aircraft off the Canadair production line. Karachi/Faisal AFB holds a further four or more CL–13s and F–86Fs and other bases maintain mainly 'Fs as gate guards. As far as is known, none of these aircraft have appeared in the west yet, though their use may be limited due to the fact they were withdrawn from use due to corrosion problems.

It is doubtful if any Sabres of the **Peruvian Air Force**/*Fuerza Aerea del Peru (FAP)* still exist. Now operating mainly Soviet manufactured equipment, the *FAP* operated 15 ex USAF F–86Fs from 1955. Replacing P–47D Thunderbolts the Sabres served with the Grupo de Caza 12 at Limatambo. Incredibly, 12 survived until 1979 to be replaced by Sukhoi Su–22s. Nothing has been heard of the F–86s since and they are presumed scrapped, though Peru is a close neighbour of Bolivia . . .

The **Philippines** gained Sabre capability from 1957, with F–86Ds forming a single, all-weather fighter squadron, with another 40 F–86Fs went to equip three day fighter units. Though the D's were surplused in 1968 the F models carried on in front line service for some

Portugese air Force F–86F of the Escuadra de Caca BA–5 *in 1979* **Top** . *In complete contrast Danish air Force F–86D 18421 at Vaerlose in 1977* (**both MAP**).

time. Around 20 remaining in 1978 were formed into one reserve squadron operating out of Basa Air Force Base. However, by 1984 only three were in flyable condition at any one time and the Sabre was finally phased out of service soon after. A visit to Basa late in 1984 revealed most of the Sabres dismantled in a scrapyard near the base. Other than those still present at least one F–86F and F–86D are preserved at Nichols Air Force Base near Manilla. Any further news of these aircraft would be appreciated.

The **Portugese Air Force** (*Forca Aerea Portuguesa*) was the last European front line user of the type. Operating some 50 F–86Fs from October 1958 these aircraft were delivered under the Mutual Defence Assistance Program (MDAP) and formed *Escuadrons* 51 and 52 at Ota. A year later both units moved to Monte Real to form *Grupo Operacional* 501 with no separate squadrons. Finally, from the mid 1960's FAP Sabres operated within the *Escuadra de Caca* BA5. Portugal has now relied on the close proximity of Spain for much of its air defence protection and as a result did not put re-equipment high on its list of priorities. As a result, to back up the existing Sabre fleet it acquired 50 ex *Luftwaffe* CL–13s, though most of these airframes were used as a source of spares. Two F–86Fs were also acquired from Norway as mentioned earlier.

July 1970 saw the *FAP* finally withdraw its Sabre fleet. In a particularly far sighted move the *FAP* Museum placed six Sabres into store at Alverca for exchange in the future against aircraft required for their museum. One F–86F (5320) is kept in an airworthy condition at Monte Real for use at air shows. Finally, eleven can be seen in a scrap yard near the Sintra Air Base.

Surprisingly for such a minor Sabre user, many of the **Royal Saudi Air Force (RSAF)** Sabres are still extant. Not all of the 16 F–86Fs delivered entered service due to immediate spares shortages and even then guns were not fitted for some time! RSAF Sabres served from 1958 until the early 1970s with 7 Squadron at Dharan AFB where the dry desert air ensured the aircraft remained in good condition. Unfortunately, the sand has taken its toll on cockpit canopies though in general the six or seven F–86Fs which survive are well preserved. All can be seen at Dharan where two are preserved, the remainder lying in a scrapyard.

The **South African Air Force (SAAF)** had the unique distinction of operating the Sabre twice, and under very different circumstances. No. 2 *Cheetah* Squadron, under the control of the United Nations, and attached to No. 18 Fighter Bomber Wing operated 22 F–86Fs from January 1953 during the Korean War. The armistice was signed just seven months later and the Sabres passed back to the U.S.A. from where most later passed to Taiwan. This brief flirtation with the Sabre must have had a lasting effect, for the *SAAF* later purchased 34 brand new Canadair Sabre 6's, in 1956. Serving again with the *Cheetahs* the CL–13s also went to equip No. 1 Squadron when the latter converted to the Mirage III in 1963. Thirteen years passed before 1 Squadron relinquished their aircraft for more modern types. In 1975 No. 85 Advanced Flying School was formed from surplus Sabres at Pietersburg and was the last *SAAF* unit to fly the type. It gave up its aircraft in April 1980.

Most of the remaining SAAF Sabres found their way to the United States, *Flight Systems Inc.,* gaining ten for their drone programme. Warbirds Worldwide member John MacGuire of Fort Hancock, Texas, now flies one of these aircraft, still in its *SAAF* markings. Six CL–13s remain in South Africa although one aircraft disappeared recently, reputedly to be shipped to France. . .

At least two of the original *SAAF* F–86Fs were passed on to the **Spanish Air Force**/*Ejercito del Aire (EdA)* to form part of an eventual procurement for 244 of the type. Reconditioned by CASA to dash 40 standard, the *EdA* Sabres were delivered to Getafe from late 1955 and initially equiped five *Escuadrons* with an additional unit formed later. During this period Spanish Sabres stood on dawn to dusk 'Zulu' alert as part of Air Defence Command, whilst gunnery training was carried out on the Delta 59 range at San Juan air base.

The arrival of F–104G Starfighters in 1965 signalled the start of the slow re-equipment process which was not complete until 1974. The last aircraft in service was C5–199 serving with *Escuadron 732*. Spain currently has at least 9 Sabres, two of which reside in the excellent *Museo del Aire* at Cuatro Vientos, near Madrid. An ex *EdA* F–86F is also registered to the Mid-Atlantic Air Museum at Reading, Pennsylvania as N51RS. News of this restoration is eagerly awaited.

Similarly operating a large number of Sabres for more than 25 years was **Taiwan**. The *Chinese Nationalist Air Force (CNAF)* gained the first of 320 RF(Photo Recce) and F–86Fs from 1955. Among these aircraft was 12910, previously a Korean war veteran and the personal mount of Ace Joseph McConnell and named *Beautious Butch* II. McConnell gained five of his 16 MiG kills in this aircraft. Sadly it was later written off in *CNAF* service. F–86Ds were used in limited numbers by the *CNAF* but were replaced by the F–100 in 1960. F–86Fs

were fitted with Aero 3B missile rails which enabled the AAM.N7 missile (later named Sidewinder) to be carried. *CNAF* Sabres gained the distinction of being the first aircraft to use them in combat. From August 1958, Red Chinese MiG–17s were engaged over the Formosa Straits and in a two month period 29 enemy jets were downed for no reported losses to the Sabres. Even when hostilities died down CNAF F–86s stood alert with 2 wings until F–100s took over the role in the 1960s.

As late as 1977 No. 2 and 3 Wings operated almost 100 F–86Fs, though F–5Es were begining to replace them. When, finally the *CNAF* bid farewell to their Sabres, two squadrons of the Taiwan Air Reserve took over the surviving machines and saw them into the 1980s. It is quite possible that they are still flying but approaches to the authorities have proven fruitless in ascertaining this. Nonetheless, Taiwan must present itself as a great untapped source of Sabre spares if nothing else. Had 12910 survived, I can guarantee that at least one F–86 would have found its way home!

Still in Asia, the **Royal Thai Air Force (RTAF)** operated 40 F–86Fs from 1961 until 1966 when F–5s replace them. 12 Squadron began operating 20 F–86Ls from 1964 and these again were replaced by late model F–5s. Thailand was the only export customer for the F–86L which was a major update version based on the F–86D. 827 aircraft were modified from 1956. Extended wing span, similar to those of the dash 40 F model and an on-board computer which received and processed ground radar data were the main features of the conversion. *RTAF* received these aircraft from the USAF inventory. Six F–86Fs and four F–86Ls remain in Thailand, of which eight are in the Bangkok area, notably at the *RTAF Museum* (one of each) Liumpini Park (F–86F) and the *RTAF* Academy (one of each). Two F's are also in use as decoys at Don Muang air base.

F–86F serial C5–235: it would appear a new nose section has been installed on the aircraft (**MAP**).

The Sensational Sabre

Another country which has operated the Sabre is **Tunisia**. Initially gaining use of 15 ex USAF F–86Fs in 1969 these were replaced by Macchi MB326Ks in 1978. However, another batch of around a dozen F models were delivered 'from storage in Arizona' in 1983 and these may well have been Japanese aircraft returned to the USA under the agreements of the MAP.

The **Turkish Air Force**/*Turk Hava Kuvvetleri (THK)* operated a wide variety of Sabres from July 1954 when 102 CL–13 Mk 2s brought up to Mk. 4 standard and redesignated F–86E(M) were delivered from Canada. These aircraft formed the core of Nos. 141, 142 and 143 Squadrons providing fighter cover over Turkey. Twelve F–86Fs followed in 1958 by which time the spares situation was becoming acute despite the support from Canadair. Amidst the confusion some 50 F–86Ds were delivered and partly took over from the F–86E(M)s and F–86Fs at Merzifon and Eskisehir.

Thirty F–86Ks followed in 1964, reportedly from Holland, though the latter only ever returned eight Sabres. The F–86E/F squadrons served until 1966 whilst four units flying the "D" and "K" models soldiered on until 1969. Most of the *THK* aircraft were then scrapped and only four "E" models remain in Turkey. Two are preserved at the *THK* Museum at Ataturk.

The Sabres use in the **United Kingdom**, at the hands of the *Royal Air Force* is well documented. In short 430 CL–13s, supplied in Mk 2 and Mk 4 configuration served with the RAF as Sabre F.1 and F.4 respectively. From May 1953 CL–13s were deployed with ten squadrons in West Germany and two more at home.

By the summer of 1956 all RAF Sabres had been phased out with Italy and Yugoslavia receiving the majority of these aircraft. Some derelict Sabres remained in the UK as late as 1974 at Ascot and Lasham though none no longer exist. However XB733 survived and is currently with T. Bracewell after periods of ownership with *HAPS* at Biggin Hill and *Reflectaire* at Blackpool. Registered G–ATBF the machine has suffered much corrosion but would make a challenging restoration project.

Briefly, in the late 1970s, four ex *Luft-waffe* Canadair Sabres arrived at Wroughton in Wiltshire for the late Ormond Haydon-Baillie. One of these was earmarked for rebuild to flying condition but the tragic death of Haydon-Baillie in a Cavalier Mustang put paid to the project and the Sabres were sold to *Flight Systems Inc.* in the United States and are still flying there, distinguishable by their Martin Baker ejector seats and modified canopy mechanisms.

The Sabre served widely with the **United States Air Force**; space prevents inclusion of details in this article.

Mojave in California is the home of **Flight Systems Inc.** Since the mid 1970's *FSI* have been converting mainly ex RCAF CL–13s to drone configuration for the U.S. Army. These QF–86Es were delivered from 1977 and 36 had been ordered by 1980. *FSI* Sabres normally operate from Holloman AFB in New Mexico over the White Sands missile range to be destroyed by a wide variety of ordnance. *FSI* also have a fleet of manned CL–13s which, amongst other duties, provide target towing facilities. The ex Haydon-Baillie machines are here.

Private civilian operation of the F–86 in the United States got off to a bad start when, on 24th September 1972 a CL–13 Mk 5, registration N275X, of *Spectrum Air Inc.*, crashed off the end of the runway at Sacramento airport, careering into an ice cream parlour and killing 22 people. Pilot inexperience was recognised as the main cause of the accident.

Today, the Sabre is one of the most popular warbird jets in the United States, and for reference a table of those aircraft currently registered is listed below.

The **Fuerza Aerea Venezuela (FAV)** purchased 22 F–86Fs in 1955 and six were delivered in October 1955, the rest following later. These aircraft went into service with the *Escuadron de Caza 36 Jaguares*. *FAV* F–86Fs endured until 1972 when Mirage IIIs arrived to replace them. A year later, nine of these aircraft were sold to Bolivia. 1967 had seen the arrival of some 51 F–86Ks, purchased from the Luftwaffe to equip *Escaudron 34 Caciques* and 35 *Panteras* at Barquisimento. Four of these later went to Honduras in 1969 whilst phase out by the *FAV* occurred in the 1970s in favour of the F–5. Unconfirmed reports suggest that some of the F–86Ks stayed on until 1978, operating alongside more modern machinery. Four F–86Ks never arrived in Venezuela and remained abandoned on the island of Curacao, less than 50 miles from their destination until they were burned in 1982.

Venezuela may still hold some secrets but it is believed that only three Sabres still exist here namely an F–86F and K preserved at the Maracay museum and an F–86K at Mariscal Sucre air base.

Finally, the **West German Luftwaffe**, continuing its post war build up, initially took delivery of 75 Sabres 5s from Canadair in January 1957. These equipped the *Waffenschule 10*, basically an operational training unit, in anticipation of the follow-up order of 225 Sabre 6s. Sabres did not reach the squadrons until 1959 when *Jagdgeschwader* 71, 72 and 73 equipped with the last Canadair Sabres built. A further batch of 226 F–86Ks were ordered but by the time these started to arrive the order had been reduced to 88 and even then only 57 ever saw service here, entering service with *JG* 74 and 75, though the latter unit almost immediately disbanded. The remaining 31 K models were utilised for spares and some of these, still in natural metal finish, found their way to the *FAV*. By 1967 the Canadair Sabres had been replaced by Fiat G–91s and F–104G Starfighters, the F–86Ks also by F–104s. From mid 1966, seven Sabre 6s were operated by *Condor Flugdienst* for towing aerial gunnery targets. Flying from Westerland, *Condor* replaced these aircraft in 1974 favouring the G–91 and OV10 Bronco. The CL–13s were then passed to technical school TSLW 13 at Fassberg and kept in flyable condition. One of these, D9523 is said to still fly on occasion. One ex *Luftwaffe* Sabre, c/n 1711 was registered ad D–FADE in the late 1960s though little is known about this aircraft other than it being written off near Frankfurt in 0000. As many as 45 Sabres can still be seen in West Germany, many serving as gate guards.

So it can be seen that this aircraft, with such a rich and varied history, has the prospect of a rich future in store. Thanks to the efforts of enthusiasts worldwide, the Sabre will fly on into the next century, witness to its timeless appeal.

Continued on Page 38

Pictured in 1977, CL–13 Sabre 6 350 of 85 AFS South African Air Force. (Military Aircraft Photographs).

allowed you more time to think what was going on rather than attempting a visual 'run-and-break' during your first sortie. Setting up for the descent, both throttles are at idle, and looking to be about 15 miles on the runway centreline at 2000 feet with the gears and the flap down. Heads in now and on to instruments it quickly became apparent that the aircraft was not speed-stable ie you constantly had to be aware of what the speed was doing and making small power adjustments. It was not possible, as in more modern aircraft to set an RPM and peg a speed and you constantly had to move the throttles to maintain the speed you required. Trying to pick up the scan rate between speed heading and height whilst listening to all the air traffic instructions certainly concentrated the mind. Maintaining your head in the cockpit you look up at 400 feet and decide to overshoot to join the visual circuit. Unlike most fighter aircraft you apply full power, select the airbrakes in and leave the undercarriage and flap down to minimise fatigue. At 500 feet midway down the runway you start a gentle 60° bank turn to put yourself down-wind at a thousand feet and 200 knots with the downwind checks complete. On a right hand circuit, sitting in the left hand seat you were now blind to the runway which lay on your right hand side. Now it was a case of instrument flying, holding the height on the altimeter and maintaining your runway heading, allowing for wind. Setting yourself up at the finals turnpoint, rolling in at 200–190 knots, kicking in a small amount of rudder and pulling back on the stick to keep the aeroplane going around the turn, the feature of a swept wing fighter. Half way round finals you pop the airbrakes to allow you to set a higher power setting than required – to give you the previously mentioned power to get you out of trouble if required. Getting onto the centre-line your finger is constantly trimming back to give the aircraft its characteristic stalky nose-up appearance on finals. Things are happening very fast now as you reduce the speed to 175 knots, looking to cross the fence at 165 knots and touch down on the numbers (and no-where else!) at 160 knots. A final check of your gear and flap as you now divide your attention between speed and runway. Is the threshold moving up in the windscreen? If so you are not on a collision with the threshold and something has changed. Just as you feel you are about six inches off the deck it's airbrakes IN, power UP and you overshoot. We rarely tried rolls; this saved tyre life and aircraft fatigue. Climbing away, it's straight into another circuit, could be a flapless circuit, adding ten knots to all the speeds, and taking care to avoid a tail scrape with the higher nose attitude, or maybe a simulated single engined circuit, again no problem due to the enormous surplus thrust you have available with the Avon engines. Alternatively you could undertake a low-level circuit at 500 feet as opposed to 1000 feet. Final landing and you call 'precautionary' to air traffic to let them know that should you lose your 'chute you will be staying on the deck due to the fuel remaining ie that you haven't enough fuel to do another circuit. Round finals again you make doubly sure your touch-down point is in the numbers exactly the same as before, pegging the speed between 165 and 160 knots. If you landed past the numbers at 180 knots you stood a good chance of entering the barrier due to the Lightning's poor brakes. The T.5 had no arrestor hook in case you had to use the over-run cable. Over the fence and a small check back on the stick to plant her firmly on the concrete, pulling the 'chute handle and retarding both throttles to idle whilst squeezing the brakes all at once, similar I imagine to carrier deck landings in an F-4.

Night landings in poor weather is a story in itself. Popping the 'chute killed about 10–15 knots immediately. The main difficulty came in high crosswinds on a wet runway where the slab sided fuselages and the high T-tail and thin tyres made the aircraft a real handful. Pilots would frequently appear in the crew room ashen faced after a wet, windy night landing! Some pilots would tell of their experiences of having both hands on the stick, smashing the rudder from side to side just to keep their aircraft straight on the runway.

Back to the LTF, average sortie time for the T.5 was between 30 and 35 minutes, and it normally required five of these sorties prior to your first solo in an F.3. This could often take some time as you had to have flown the T.5 on the same day in suitable weather conditions with a minimal cloud base and good visibility and as low a cross wind as possible. Without stating the obvious, it was a real shock to find yourself on your own, with no one to give you that last bit of advice for the landing and no one to remind you to check fuel, or assist you if you had an emergency. As you taxi out you go through your pre-take off checks several times just to re-assure yourself that all was well. Lined up on the threshold you

Classic Lightning pose; Wing Commander Spencer's personal aircraft hurtles skyward (**Ian Black**).

glanced back over either shoulder and you can see very little, only the in-flight refuelling probe on your left hand side and the highly swept wings. Once you are airborne in a single seater, there is only one person that can land the beast – and that is YOU! As it transpires the landing is not too bad as you have just had a consolidated effort in the two-seater, building up on your circuits. The tricky part comes in the radar phase when your mind is still full of figures, heights and headings from the last intercept. Then comes the difficult part; trying to land the aircraft with all that information in your head.

The CONVEX part of the LTF course was about 25 to 30 sorties – five to go solo, after which max rate turning, supersonic performance, a large bout of instrument flying culminating in an IRT (Instrument Rating Test) giving you a 'white'

no target evasion and known target heading with targets above the fighter at preset speeds. However, within six months the pilot would be expected to deal with any evasion in heading, height or speed. Early sorties provided an extremely high workload; attempting to fly the aircraft whilst having your head stuck in the radar tube and managing the weapons system and the fuel system required a new and unfound skill. To achieve a simulated weapons kill on radar was no mean feat. However, visual identification on radar was an even harder skill.

The Lightnings main task during peacetime was to identify targets, unknown, day or night, 365 days a year. The vis-ident procedure involved closing to a target to about a mile (on radar again) and then gently easing in to 300 yards again on radar simulating in cloud or at

sighted the Lightning was pure fun to fly and fight. If a target was sighted at long range a small nudge on the throttles would quickly give you a mass of overtake and bring you into missile range in seconds. A late pick-up meant converting excess speed to angles; this was done either pulling to the G limit or, weather permitting reefing the aircraft into the vertical to convert speed to height and thus allow better turn-rate from low speed at height. Most squadron pilots attempted to use only 'cold' power at low-level; this had a two-fold bonus. It kept down the noise and reduced fuel consumption. In addition to low-level evasion training over land, similar training over the sea was also carried out on the LTF. This would be most useful for the squadron work-up where most intercepts were carried out over the North Sea.

rating using a decision height of 400 feet, then close formation (which was a delight), battle, low-level, and then tail-chasing. Finally a few more general handling trips and then a final handling test. This really covered everything learned so far with some sort of simulated emergency near the end of the sortie which required a diversion to a local airfield. Having passed your final handling test it was back to ground school for a weeks lectures prior to the radar phase.

Prior to any of the radar sorties lengthy briefings were given on the weapons system – either *Red Top* or *Firestreak* (the gun was left to individual squadrons however as no LTF aircraft carried them). Additionally, many hours were devoted to basic radar theory, intercept technique and aircraft performance. As much use of the simulator was made as possible with each sortie flown in the simulator prior to being flown in the air. Initial radar sorties were very basic with

night to pick up a target visually to join in close formation on him – no mean feat on a single seat aircraft.

Towards the middle of the radar phase on the LTF a night dual sortie was followed by a night solo – this being introduced to give a taste of squadron operations. With about 30 radar sorties (approximately 20 hours completed) the fun part of the course began with low-level evasion training and like ACT ie Lightning V Lightning Air Combat Training.

Having come from the Hawk the major plus of the Lightning at low-level was its enormous thrust, something it had a staggering amount of. It was all too easy to go supersonic at low-level, and a constant eye had to be kept on the speed, fuel and position. Fighting the aeroplane at low-level overland was back to the 'fifties'. Folding the radar 'boot' away and reverting to mark one eyeball to detect hostile targets. Once a hostile target was

If the weather was unsuitable for low-level flying the course would switch into air combat mode with students using a safety height of 10,000 feet as a base. If pilots new to the Lightning were surprised by the low-level fuel consumption air combat took the biscuit. In full reheat sortie times in an F.3 from take-off to landing could often be as low as ten minutes. Having had your appetite whetted for most types of Lightning flying the course culminated in an OPEVAL - an operational evaluation of your ability, whereby any aspect of the previous months flying could be tested in a single sortie. A typical sortie could entail a high level intercept, to a visual identification, descent to low-level for another radar intercept followed by close formation recovery through cloud for a pairs landing, all with only 40 hours on type!

Having passed the OCU and feeling almost like a fighter pilot you quickly

Colour photographs opposite: (both by Ian Black) *Top: Lightning T.5 XV328 in* Lightning Training flight *Colours. This is one of six aircraft procured by arnie Glass, and it is currently located at Cranfield.* **Lower:** *The bosses aircraft with black spine – Single seat XR725 shows the cramped cockpit to advantage*

Continued on Page 46

Triumph and Tragedy

Raymond Guy Neeley (call sign *Biscuit*), was killed on June 4, 1987 at 6:47 a.m. on the desolate desert of Mojave, California, when he crashed while flying a Douglas A–4A Fighter/Bomber, N444AV, serial #14219. This story of the death of a fine aviator and the destruction of a warbird has lessons for all of us.

The aircraft was originally built as the very last – A model. The U.S. Congress had just funded the –B programme. Therefore, serial #14219 was equipped with some of the –B components. However, the engine was a Wright J–65–W16A. The aircraft weighed in at 8,728.90 empty. The USMC flew the aircraft for a short while and then it was sold as a gate guard.

My involvement began when the aircraft was purchased in 1983 and was transported to Chino, CA. There it was rebuilt by Guy at *Unlimited Aircraft Limited* during the years of 1983-1986. After being rebuilt, the A–4 was registered with the FAA, and was now legal to fly.

Before I met Guy, he had experienced a flameout in an A–4 at pattern altitude and had to eject to safety. The aircraft fell to its destruction a few hundred yards from the runway. The A–4's high key is at 7,000ft AGL. At this magic altitude, you barely have enough time to make one 180 degree course reversal and plant your main gear on the numbers. There is no room for error. You either make it or you don't! Once your sink rate escalates, you cannot make a successful ejection to safety. I often wonder whether Guy was

A. Pascal Mahvi tells of his experience of flying the Skyhawk, how his close friend Guy Neeley was killed and the lessons to be learned from his tragic death.

thinking about that flameout on June 4.

When it crashed, the A4–A was being used to shoot a commercial for a Japanese oil company. The production company needed the aircraft to be dressed up with a nose mounted long pitot tube. Don't ask why! The aircraft looked like it sported a refueling probe — only it was in the wrong place! They also wanted the aircraft painted in grey and blue. Guy completed the pilot job in Ontario on May 29th and asked me to fly the A–4 to California City for the final preparation.

The departure, as always, was very exciting. I mounted my rocketship, strapped in, and fired up the beast. Taxiing down the long taxiway at Ontario was discouraging. The combination of the A–4's big tail and small wheel base makes for an interesting taxi experience in crosswinds; it is like riding a bar of soap on your kitchen floor.

Once cleared for takeoff, I managed to make an uninterrupted climb through the ARSA to 16,500ft in one fell swoop. It's interesting to see how fast ATC works with you when your aircraft type is an A–4! Level at 16.5, I reduced to 98% power. In no time I was indicating Mach 0.9 and arrived at my destination within minutes.

Northwest of Edwards, I dropped down to the deck and I trekked across to the

north end of the airport flying a tight one mile arc to the threshold. The low pass must have been spectacular. At the departure end a slight aft pressure on the stick produced a balistic climbing turn to right downwind. Speed brakes and gear down abeam the numbers. Flaps down. Donut captured all the way down to the narrow runway. It looked like a carrier deck!

As I arrived at the ramp, my fan club was there to greet my arrival. There was one problem. I could not get down easily. The cockpit sits about 10 feet off the ground. A pickup truck had to be recruited to carefully bring the hero down to earth.

The production company used the aircraft for ground shots for a few days. Then, on June 4 at dawn, the crew gathered at Mojave air terminal to discuss that day's flight. No one really was prepared for what was in store in forty-seven minutes. Because Guy is dead, no one can know exactly what took place, and I was not present. What follows, therefore, is necessarily a speculative reconstruction of what happened.

During the pilot briefing, Guy was asked to roll the aircraft over a speeding Ferrari, while the camera car gave chase from behind! In order to remain in frame for the camera car, the roll had to occur very close to the speeding Ferrari. There was no margin for error. Because of the A–4A slow flight characteristics, this manoeuvre involves a high degree of risk. I witnessed this trait during the shooting of the *Top Gun/Diet Pepsi* commercial.

The briefing over, Guy strapped

himself to the A–4 and taxied away. Immediately, after takeoff, he rolled the aircraft low over the runway and made a steep climb for left downwind. The ensuing low pass was at high speed and produced a graceful roll. Minutes later, he was on station, a mile east of California City.

The Ferrari raced northward along the road close to 200 MPH. The plan apparently was for Guy to dive for the Ferrari, and once directly overhead, to arrest his aircraft's movement in relation to the automobile. Speed control in such a case was of paramount importance, and my friend had mastered his trade. The camera crew followed from behind gathering test shots.

At the end of the road, the Ferrari coasted down while Guy would reverse course using a bastardized Immelman, to suit his need. He flew to his station and awaited the ground crews and the Ferrari's arrival to the starting point. This was repeated twice.

At the end of the third pass, Guy elected to perform a Wifferdill, turning right 90° first, followed by a left 270°. Upon completion of the course reversal, he was found flying southbound, west of the road, low to the ground. Six ex-USAF type police witnesses saw him pick up the nose and enter a roll. At the 180° point, one wing tip is said to have hit a dense bush followed by a tail strike. Guy managed to level the aircraft by completing the roll.

Guy then pulled the alternate ejection handle located between his thighs. The seat must have made it halfway out of the cockpit. At that instant, the cockpit hit the ground at approximately 30 G's. The seat, Guy, and the burning rocket slammed back into the cockpit, causing the rocket to explode, catapulting Guy into the air. The cockpit came apart from the internal explosion. My dearest friend was dead before being thrown clear of the aircraft. This is said to have occurred at 6:47 a.m. I pray he had been spared the pain. But those of us alive that knew him, still mourn his death.

Due to the recent birth of my son, I had decided against joining Guy the evening of June 3. Instead, I spent the night at home. Unbeknownst to Guy, my plan was to join him on June 4 at about 10:00 a.m. for brunch. That early morning, the telephone rang, shattering the tranquility within our home. I picked up the receiver and heard Steve Neeley's measured and controlled voice at the other end, "Pascal . . . I have some very bad news. Guy has crashed the A–4 and he was killed" I shall never forget the emptiness and anger that swept over me. I cried out . . . out of control. My wife and I hugged each other in tears and shock. Steve made sure to ask me not to fly myself to location. Of course, he was right.

It took three hours to round up a pilot and aircraft. Then it took an hour to get to California City. Once overhead, I saw a long charred trail along the sand, terminated by a mangled aircraft. The aircraft itself was not visible to my teary eyes. I believed that there was nothing left. I gasped for air in order to fight my tears, but to no avail.

Once on the ground, a TV station helicopter flew over to pick me up and took me to the wreckage. We landed in a clearing surrounded by tall bushes. They reached the height of the rotorhead. Could Guy have had an optical illusion over this vast desert? Once Steve saw me, he ran over and ushered me away from the reporters. He described to me what he saw, in what appeared to be a calm collected fashion. Inside, I knew he was ready to explode. I was in tears and trembling from anger. I wanted my friend back.

It is deduced that once straight and level, the aircraft panned out and had hit tail first and then nosed over. The cockpit slammed down forcing the seat back in to the cockpit and exploding the rocket. Everything forward of the fuselage fuel tank came apart. The cockpit was found in six pieces; canopy, nose, left half, right half, seat bulkhead, and the charred seat. Then the aircraft simply rolled up into a fireball and came to rest some 100 or so feet ahead of Guy's body. The engine was found by the NTSB to have produced full power on impact, where the shock seized the compressor and proceeded to melt down. Likewise, the throttle and fuel control was also found at military power. My dear friend's first reaction had been to try to regain control. Instead, he lost his life because he initiated the ejection process a couple of seconds late. Ironically, six hours after Guy's death, I learned that my wife was pregnant.

I met Guy at *Unlimited Aircraft Limited* an outfit based in Chino, CA. Over the years, I had become close friends with the owner, Mr. Bruce Goessling. Due to Bruce's relationship with him, Guy and I had developed a very close relationship of our own. Because we flew together, this friendship was forged in steel in a very few short months. Guy was hired by Bruce to build the A–4A.

Guy and I flew two Canadair T–33s, the second purchased from Bruce in 1985. That aircraft was intended to be Guy's ship for a two man T–33 formation at airshows. We flew the two T–33's all over the U.S. in 1986. We covered some 8,000 miles and visited some 30 airports, zig zagging across the land and ending up in Oshkosh. We saw the nation in style. But that is yet another story.

We flew together every chance we got; often over the objection of our wives! Guy taught me manoeuvres learned in the military. I shall cherish the experience forever. As a civilian, I learned tactical manoeuvres as well as other fun things, such as close formation (IFR and VFR) and fighter jet aerobatics. The experience made me a better pilot. My abilities grew by leaps and bounds.

He was one tough instructor. Very exacting and demanding in every sense of the word. I remember Guy running me through the drill in order to prepare me for the A–4 FAA checkride in May of 1987. We locked ourselves up in my conference room for two days. We talked systems and numbers until I was blue in the face.

My first A–4 ride was at Mojave. We reviewed systems while I was seated in the cockpit. I then asked Guy to step down. Prior to start, I asked him to please take good care of my wife should I encounter misfortune and not return alive. I was not joking. I was very serious, as I consider flying serious business. The possibility did exist that I could not handle such a hotrod. I had never been in command of a sweptwing aircraft, let alone a delta platform called an A–4A! But I had adequate training under the wings of two very capable aviators, Capt. Ross Diehl and Guy Neeley. Besides, I had faced death before and I believe that I could take this calculated risk. In any event, I had drafted my will prior to this day! Moreover, I somewhat undertand my limitations.

He gave me a confident look and the traditional "thumbs up". I started up and after checking all flight controls, taxied away. I remember missing Steve Neeley, our crew chief. He is professional in attitude. He had all the hand signals down pat and guided you through the flight control checks as if you were a member of the *Blue Angels*. Then, prior to your taxi, he would come to attention giving you a very crisp salute. He plain made you feel great. Guy, on the other hand, was a fighter pilot, not a crew chief! He haphazardly pointed at your flight control surfaces and then waved "see you later, bud!"

He had wanted me to taxi around for a while in order to get used to the ground handling qualities, and extremely sensitive brakes. I complied to a point. That point presented itself very quickly at the end of the taxiway. I had to takeoff. Guy had been following me in Dan Sabovich's Cadillac. I announced my intentions and was greeted with utter silence! I could hear Guy's heart pounding and praying to God to preserve his sanity. I was about to launch myself into the wild blue with a hot airplane I had never flown. And I was told in physics class what goes up must come down. In flight school, I learned it's supposed to be in a controlled fashion! What might he say to my wife if . . .!
I had one big question on my mind: Could I handle this hotrod? The question vanished the minute I completed the takeoff checklist and advanced the throttle to 80% while holding the brakes. The roar of the engine filled the cockpit. The aircraft nose compressed itself downward on to the nose gear strut, flattening the nose gear tyre. I could sense that I was calm. My heartbeat had not accelerated. I was

Continued on Page 26

COLOUR CENTRE SPREAD (All photographs Thierry Thomassin). Top Left: *Spectacular view of the A–4.* **Bottom Left:** *N444AV in company with the black T–33.* **Top Right:** *With everything down the Skyhawk looks every bit a naval machine.* **Bottom Right:** *Pascal Mahvi formates on the B–25 camera ship. Guy Neeley is in the rear seat.*

Strapping the A–4 on prior to take off. **(Thierry Thomassin).**

not afraid! It was time for brake release.

Brake release and military power launched me down the runway at an ever increasing speed. At Vr1 I was on my way. Gear was selected up. Flaps followed. Speed built up to 250 kts in no time. Power was backed off to 98%. The speed kept increasing, so I picked up the nose.

Skyward I went at an ever increasing high angle! I was riding a hotrod alright. Thinking back, I could swear I was near vertical. But, I know it's impossible . . . I was not in an F–14. However, at 17,000 feet, I pulled back the stick further until my world was upside down, arresting my rocket climb prior to reaching the Positive Control Area (I have often wondered how the ATC radar depicts such a maneeouvre on the radar screen. It must be a stationary dot with an increasing altitude read out during the climb). I rolled the aircraft rightside up and reduced power. I tried to reach the roll limits of the aircraft. Instead, I kept coming in contact with the sides of the canopy.

I had never encountered such sensitivity in the roll axis. This A–4A, although built with many of the dash B components, had a single hydraulic system. The dash A model has a stick extension that slides out to give the pilot better leverage on the flight controls in case of hydraulic failure. When in the retracted position, the grip is about level with the pilot's thighs. The upper part (the grip) does have a very slight play within the lower tube. In rolling and turning the aircraft, all that was required was a slight twist of the upper stick. This action caused the lower part to move a degree or two toward the required turn. The resultant roll was unbelievable. I moved about the sky with such energy and grace.

Bingo fuel was upon me in no time. I now had to worry about getting this beast on the ground, in one piece. It would take at least two tries.

Down I came practising the capture of my donut on my angle of attack system. On my first attempt, I lost the donut. On the second try I locked onto that baby all the way to landing and did a touch-and-go. The third go was a level high speed flyby, followed by a full stop landing.

Both of us were exhausted, but elated with joy. I had just flown the A–4A; Guy had just shared his "raison d'etre" with a friend. The sharing of such experiences brings guys close together. We made plans to take the aircraft to various airshows. Alas, they were short lived. I flew the aircraft a total of 10 wonderful hours.

Folks, Guy was a great *pilot*. Just ask around. He was trained in the military to fly to combat standards. Guy was a 5,000 hour pilot of which 1,000 hours was combat flying time in A–4s, in Vietnam. Guy enlisted in to the USMCR and was dispatched by it to the OCS at Quantico, Virginia as well as to the USAF at Valdosta, Georgia, for initial flight training. Once he received his USAF wings, he was dispatched to the USN at Yuma, Arizona, for Naval flight training. Upon receiving his Navy wings, he was attached to the Marine Corps VMA 223 and dispatch to Vietnam as a USMC captain. There, he was recommended and received *nineteen* Air Medals with an Oak Leaf Cluster for heroic action in combat. Guy never talked about his medals to me. I learned this fact only in March of 1988. I am told by his brother that upon discharge, the USMC called him to tell him of the 19th medal. He asked them to just to drop it in the mail. This should tell you something about the

man. Guy was a highly-trained, professional combat pilot and flew just about daily. Although he had not attended college, he had educated himself. He read books and world events continuously and discussed world politics very intelligently. He was a man that fit in any situation. He dined and carried the day with the elite as well as the upper, middle and lower socio-economic backgrounds; he made everyone like him. He was a leader; and probably born as such. And he loved aircraft and people. In return, people respected him. Moreover, he was smart, warm, courteous, and a real family man. He always gave 100% of himself to a particular job. He fought for what he believed in life.

His death, at the age of 40 was senseless. At the 1987 Chino Airshow, he said to me in regards to Dave Zeuschel's accident that same year that "if you are in this business long enough, sooner or later you end up having an accident, hopefully, just to teach you a lesson". Two weeks later he was involved in an accident that took his life.

Flying these types of hot fighters is a risky business. These aircraft are designed for one purpose, to be combat fighters. They are *not* designed to be forgiving; they all have particular flight characteristics and demands, and the pilot better know and observe the aircraft's traits as well as the pilot's limitations. Especially if you are a Sunday warrior, as he and I and the rest of you in civilian clothes are. The military trains daily for this risky business. The risk of dying goes with the job. To stack the odds in their favour, the military pilots are equipped with the latest and the best money can buy. A military pilot would bail out of his government issued aircraft the instant trouble developed, because of the aircraft is expendable. There is no *psychological attachment* between pilot and *aircraft*.

We, on the other hand fly warbirds on weekends. In most cases, such aircraft costs a lot of bucks and is self insured. I can tell you that the A–4 destroyed on June 4 was worth about $500,000. Guy and I talked about the psychological factor a dozen times in order to make sure we *both* understood *the aircraft is expendable*. An A–4 is not an airplane to dead stick in. It flies about as well as the space shuttle. One way ticket . . . straight down like a bloody rock.

These facts must dictate the practice of extreme caution. Guy made a fatal mistake by hesitating to eject. So did countless others who are no longer here to tell their story. Think about this next time you takeoff and decide to do something along the lines of *Top Gun*.

I can tell you that Guy and I flew by the book and conducted every flight with the greatest of care and professionalism. Our programme included first class maintenance, first class training (to include aerobatics, formation flight, altitude chamber, live fire ejection seat training and night vision training). Here money was not spared. And yet, this 5,000 hour pro was beaten by the very aircraft he commissioned! No matter how hard we trained, we were not military pilots and we knew it. We used the jargon, dressed like military pilots, and used all the

manoeuvres. But we were civilian pilots.

The message is simple and it is addressed to all civilian pilots around the world: Care about what you do. Do not fly with bad equipment. Do not fly without adequate sleep. Do not fly without your mind. Remember your limitations. You are not *Top Gun*! Moreover, you are not in the movies. You are a civilian pilot. Above all, remember not to abuse the privilege bestowed upon you as a civilian fighter pilot. Guy Neeley a combat-seasoned professional pilot, with thousands of hours of experience in fighters that you and I dream of, did lose. You can also. You and I have to put aside our egos and remember this when we fly. If this article saves one tragic death from occurring, I know my friend will smile, wherever he is today.
© **Pascal A. Mahvi.**

Californian sunshine. It was one of two such aircraft painted in these colours. Pascal is in the front seat with the late Guy Neeley in the rear seat. Shot from a B–25 Mitchell by **Warbirds Worldwide** *Chief Photographer* **Thierry Thomassin**, *May 1985 (air to air shot).*

Flying the CAC Sabre

The sleek tiger tailed Macchi jet from No 2 Operational Conversion Unit tucked in close on the starboard side. "No fuel or hydraulic leaks that I can see" was the report from Flight Lieutenant Ian Thompson, at the controls. "Roger, setting climb power". And so, the post reconstruction test flight of Avon Sabre A94–983 was underway. It was 26th March 1981, just ten days before the RAAF's 60th Anniversary Airshow to be held at Amberley, Queensland.

Time was of the essence in preparing 983 because of a relatively late decision to fly it in the Airshow, the length of time it had spent sitting in crates in a hangar and the seeming lack of spares. The dedicated few, under the leadership of Squadron Leader John Clarkson at the

George Radny, Corporal Col Foggo and many others, identities one and all, ensured 983 became a going concern on 26 March 1981.

Following a compass swing and with the assistance of one my former Sabre students to cast an eye over 983 for signs of troubles after take off, the test flight began. The rudimentary hydraulic servo flight controls felt unrefined after the Mirage on which I had spent most of my 'time' since leaving Sabres in 1971. However, the Sabre was an 'honest' aircraft – totally conventional in its handling and after a couple of minutes I felt quite at home.

Having been one of the last RAAF Sabre instructors and, in 1981 the chief Mirage instructor at No 2 Operational

in equivalent configuration could stay with a Mirage in a climb provided the Mirage did not use afterburner. A climb schedule of 400 knots into Mach 0.83 was ideal for the 'clean' Sabre and to this day is compatible with most current generation fighters.

I remember we used to think nothing of climbing to 48,000 feet in Malaysia and Thailand in the sixties to 'top' the cumulonimbus clouds which often dictated the style of our operations. By modern standards the Sabre had an unsophisticated gunsight range radar with no capability for guiding the pilot clear of areas of thunderstorms.

It was basic fighter flying – sense the aircraft's performance by the sounds it made, the feel of the controls and most of

The moment of truth; the then Squadron Leader David Leach straps '983' on for the test flight, assisted by Corporal Col Foggo, 26th March 1981 (**RAAF Official**).

RAAF's No 2 Aircraft Depot at Richmond had worked tirelessly on their labour of love and in spite of all impediments old 983 would be ready.

Although it was now officially on the RAAF aircraft register again, 983 was not to become a fully operational aircraft so the radar, gunsight and weapons circuitry was ignored. Similarly, the two 30 mm Aden guns which in the past had served the aircraft so well for air to air and air to ground gunnery were retained in a non-functioning state as ballast. All that was needed was a serviceable airframe, engine and a means of communicating with the world outside. The last was to prove more difficult to achieve than you might expect due to a break in the aircraft's aerial which went undetected. However, the efforts of Warrant Officer 'Curley' Boyes, Flight Sergeant

Group Captain David Leach, RAAF, details the first post-rebuild test flight of the RAAF Historic Flight's CAC built Sabre.

Conversion Unit at Williamtown, I guess the decision on who should fly 983 was a relatively simple one. I know there were many envious 'knucks' around and jokes were made about the broken leg I was about to get. But I had been in the right place at the right time as the saying goes.

It certainly was great to get back into an aircraft where you could look directly behind and the roomy 50's style fighter cockpit was in marked contrast to the confined business end of the Mirage. Performancewise 983 was no slouch either, and about five minutes after take off I was at 25,000 feet. The Avon Sabre was one of the 'hottest' Sabres built and

all by the seat of your pants. Eyes were always outside the cockpit. 'You could not fight what you could not see' students were told. Throughout Sabre training they heard, 'lookout, lookout, lookout . . . report the bogey' until it became second nature. To some extent those skills have been lost, superceded by the techniques of radar which extends the range of detection but at the sacrifice of field of view. Eyes out was the order of the day at 25,000 feet in 983 – what a great feeling.

Normally test flights required a climb to 40,000 feet. However, on this occasion I elected not to go that high because the radio, transponder and ADF had failed and the canopy seal had blown out – 983 was no longer pressurized. For high altitude unpressurized flight it is necessary to pre-breath 100% oxygen for a

Flying the CAC Sabre

period before getting airborne to avoid the 'bends' and besides, 25,000 feet was more than enough to show 983 off to the public in 10 days time.

All that remained before returning to base were some aerobatic manoeuvres to check the handling characteristics. I had long forgotten what a dream the Sabre was to loop and roll with its gently swept wing which captured the best of the straight wing characteristics while retaining the speed advantages of the swept wing configuration. Probably its only vice was a tendency to yaw 10–15 degrees to the right approaching the stall accompanied by a roll to the right. A spin could result if the controls were not handled correctly. Having checked the aircraft through +4G to – 1G, the RAAF imposed limits to preserve 983's airframe, it was time to think of home.

Richmond's overcast sky had enough holes to allow me to use the time tested navigation techinque of heading, airspeed and time, and map reading to locate the airfield. As I approached, Ian Thompson in the Macchi came alongside again this time for some photographs and another visual inspection before landing.

Neither of us knew that 983 was about to test our knowledge of emergency undercarriage lowering procedures.

The undercarriage had been successfully cycled several times at 10,000 feet as part of the airtest, but on down selection for landing the starboard main landing gear indicated unsafe. Flight manual undercarriage emergency extension procedures also failed to rectify the problem. With fuel now low, the decision was made to land and test the strength of the undercarriage which visually appeared to Ian Thompson to be down and locked. Ten knots was added to the normal threshold speed 'for mum and the kids' and to give better aileron control response should the undercarriage leg inadvertently fold up.

All's well that ends well and without incident 983 was returned to the Aircraft Depot with a long list of rectifications. Notwithstanding, the dedicated enthusiasts were all smiles having witnessed the fruits of their labour and a large percentage of RAAF Richmond's population had also gathered to watch the event.

The next day 983 flew again. This time with a clean bill of health. On 29 March,

just three days after its first test flight, it was a star performer at the Scholfield's Airshow.

On 5 April 1981, 983 performed at RAAF Base Amberley at the RAAF's 60th Anniversary Airshow before the admiring eyes of many who had in the past been privileged to fly the Avon Sabre. One former RAAF Officer whose enthusiasm and foresight had saved 983 from an aircraft junk yard many years earlier and who unofficially flew it before it again became a RAAF registered aircraft was also in the audience. His name is displayed on the port cowling as a continuing tribute, to Wing Commander Mick Parer.

Group Captain David Leach is now the RAAF Commander of the Northern Area based in Darwin. During his 24 years of service he has flown such types as the Mirage, Vampire, Macchi and Starfighter in addition of course to the Sabre. The Editor would like to express his thanks to Group Captain Leach and to Squadron Leader Peter Allen of the RAAF Museum at Point Cook for their help in the preparation of this article.

SABRE A94–983

Sabre A94–983 was built at the Commonwealth Aircraft Corporation factory at Fishermens Bend, Melbourne, Victoria in 1957. It had its maiden flight in November 1957 and after three weeks test flying at the Aircraft Research and Development Unit Laverton, was allotted to No 78 (Fighter) Wing on 22 April 1958 as a reserve aircraft. In November 1958, '983' was ferried to RAAF Butterworth Malaysia and went into Service with No 3 Squadron RAAF. On 5 February 1959, the aircraft sustained extensive damage to the underside fuselage and wings and subsequent internal damage from foam sprayed to quell the resulting fire.

The aircraft was returned to Australia in 1959 and after extensive repairs were completed at Commonwealth Aircraft Corporation at Avalon Victoria, was allotted to No 76 Squadron. After a period of Service with No 76 Squadron, '983'

underwent an 'E' servicing (major overhaul) At No 3 Aircraft Depot, Amberley, Queensland and on completion in March 1963, was transported to No 78 Fighter Wing, Malaysia.

In 1967, '983' returned to Australia and service with No 2 (Fighter) Operational Conversion Unit, Williamtown, NSW. October 1968 saw '983' undergo another 'E' servicing at No 3 Aircraft Depot and return to No 2 (F) OCU. June 1970 saw the aircraft allotted to No 5 Operational Training Unit until November 1971, when it was ferried to Base Squadron Butterworth as one of the 16 Sabres supplied to Malaysia by the Australian Government under the Foreign Aid Programme. '983' went into Service with No 11 Squadron Royal Malaysian Air Force as FM1983 until 1976 when it was grounded to await disposal.

In 1977 No 75 Squadron RAAF, which was stationed at Air Base Butterworth at

the time, rescued '983' from the wreckers and after a major overhaul, prepared the aircraft for another lease of life. A large crowd gathered at the airfield to watch Wing Commander Parer, Commanding Officer of the Squadron, put '983' through a successful flight on 7 July 1978.

Malaysia officially handed the aircraft back to the RAAF and it was dismantled and transported to Australia by C130 Hercules to No 2 Aircraft Depot Richmond NSW. There, it underwent a full restoration and was returned to its original condition and was successfully test flown by Squadron Leader D. Leach on 26 March 1981. Since then it has been maintained in an airworthy condition and appears at many airshows but still keeps the pilot and maintenance crew on their toes with instances such as a flameout on landing at Bendigo Airshow in 1985. Maybe a cat with nine lives which has used a couple, but is the only CA–27 Avon Sabre Jet flying in the world.

CAC Sabre A94–983 in 1966, some 22 years ago. Worthy of note are the variety of stencils resplendant along the fuselage side. **(MAP).**

Jet Owners Unite!

The issuance of Federal Aviation Administration Action Notice A 8130.5 last February has raised more than a few warbird owners attention. There is now a movement afoot by several concerned owners to develop an acceptable plan to provide the safety and proficiency necessary to keep the warbird jets flying. The last thing we want is to find all our jets relegated to static display: there is no reason for this to happen if we all get together to submit a workable proposal to the FAA. It is my understanding that the

Action Notice has been rescinded for the present and that the jet owners are now expected to come up with a replacement. This is how it should be, for we have the expertise in this field and we had better share all our experiences so that we can ensure our survival. If you can pass on ANY information you have regarding maintenance, pilot training requirements and general operational advice please do so *IMMEDIATELY* to **JETTOPICS**, P.O. Drawer 2819, Universal City, TX 78149–1819, U.S.A. We welcome

input from everyone, worldwide!

Chuck Parnall is the column writer of *JETTOPICS* which appears regularly in *WARBIRDS WORLDWIDE*. We urge all operators and indeed anyone with suggestions on training, maintenance etc. to contact Chuck with their input soonest – *Paul Coggan.*

Fouga Fever!

Fouga CM170 serial FM39 is seen here being flown by Captain Al Liusuaara on 24th May 1977. Some eleven years later the aircraft is being operated on the United States civil register as N17JV, owned by Ohio Associated Enterprises Inc. **(Hannu Valtonen)**.

The Fouga Potez CM175 Magister is a tandem, two seat basic trainer. Remarkably, the prototype first flew on July 23rd 1952. The type is still in service with several Air Forces though the disposal of several aircraft by Finland, France and more recently Belgium has provided large numbers for warbird operators. The Finnish Air Force machines were acquired by *Aces High* in the UK and *Consolidated Aviation Enterprises* in the U.S.A. though all aircraft were shipped to the U.S.A. Oshkosh, Wisconsin based *Basler Flight Services* have been importing the French machines. More recently, North Weald based *Aces High* have declared they will be importing several ex Belgian Air Force Magisters to the UK with the possibility of a Magister flying training programme being operated from there.

Several aircraft are also based in France, though because the type is still in service there it is impossible to operate one as a warbird at this time. One of these aircraft is owned by J. Lutringer who now takes up the story.

Some thirty-six years after the prototypes first flight the Fouga CM170 is still in service with the *Armee de L'Air*. Furthermore the beautiful shape of this jet, with the distinctive butterfly tail is very popular in France due to its operation, some years ago, by the *Patrouille de France*. This team operated the type for 16 years; eleven aircraft flying in formation!

Some Magisters are now available to the warbird movement in France. Ours came from the 30eme *Escadre de Chasse* (Fighter Squadron) based at Reims. She is serialled *31* and has remained in a good airworthy condition after some thirty-

The Fouga CM170 Magister is being imported to the U.S.A. in increasing numbers and is proving to be a popular choice for many warbird operators. **J.C. Lutringer** details one such machine in France and the Editor takes a general look at the type.

two years of service life as a trainer and liaison aircraft. Operating the Magister does not create any huge problems because it does not incorporate the many very sophisticated systems generally found in more complex types. There is no power controls (except from Magister number 160 on which powered ailerons have been added), no ejection seats, no reheat, and the Turbomeca *Marbore IIF* engines could not be simpler, with just one compressor (centrifugal) and one turbine wheel. Even for the more difficult maintenance tasks it is easy to find competent mechanics and large quantities of spare parts are readily available.

With no real maintenance or parts problems we can consider flying the aircraft. The pre-flight inspection is particularly easy to perform, the aircraft sitting low to the ground, getting into the cockpit does not require any ladders. There is a conveniently located folding footstep on the fuselage flank. The cockpit is typical of 1960s technology with dark colours used everywhere. Each pilot uses his parachute as a cushion for the seat. No G-suit ancilliaries have been installed except for former *Patrouille de France* aircraft which also incorporate a negative G harness directly anchored to the cabin floor. Other specified *PDF* equipment includes accelerometers

placed in various locations, and a reinforced main wing spar for continuous high-G operations. The rear pilot (the instructor) has a direct view of the pilot in front's flying helmet! So a periscope has been installed to improve forward visibility, but the system takes some getting used to before it can be used to advantage (ie without paralaxic problems). The two crew members are separated only by the two oxygen bottles.

The non-automatic start procedure requires some coordination because each sequence must be done manually and at the right time! You must start the left engine first as it drives the single generator. After speeding up the turbine with the electric starter the fuel low pressure cock is smoothly and carefully opened at 1200rpm and the ignition button depressed until the 100°c turbine temperature increase is registered. Idling is about 7500rpm but 15,000rpm is set before starting the starboard engine, in order to charge the battery and make the second engine starting sequence easier.

The Magister is a nice aircraft to taxi with its low and wide track gear, and you often surprise yourself when the taxi speed builds rapidly! A full throttle take-off is not very impressive with only a mild acceleration and a lift off at 90 knots will require about 565 metres (1880ft) of runway at full gross weight (6820lbs). Surprisingly the nose-up attitude of this aircraft at lift off is seemingly more pronounced when seen from the cockpit than from the ground. With gear and flaps up (before 140kts) the recommended climb speed is 200kts IAS up to 18,000 feet and then Mach 0.42 (yes, you must familiarise yourself with the Mach numbers, this is a jet remember!).

Exotic Aircraft of Coraopolis, Pennsylvania, operate some three Magisters, including this one, seen as FM26 in the summer of 1976 at Rissala, Finland. It is now registered N16FM. (Hannu Valtonen)

Cruising at 25,000 feet with pressurization ON will give 225kts TAS and a range of about 540nm with a conservative 19000rpm on each engine. Fuel is contained in two fuselage tanks and two tip tanks with a total capacity of 216 imperial gallons. Two larger wing tip tanks can be mounted with an extra 234 gallons of fuel in order to improve the range.

The Magister has been recognised by experienced pilots as a very easy jet to fly and she is definitely not a challenge for non-military pilots. The Magister is fully aerobatic, but you must consider the under-powered engines when aerobating. The controls are very light and well harmonized although ailerons become very heavy at high airspeeds for aircraft without powered controls. Visibility is good from each cockpit with the wing positioned aft of the cabin. The rear occupant must perform some periscopic operations in order to see ahead, but it is certainly just a matter of getting used to the system. Instructors have been proving this for years, by landing the Magister from the rear cockpit!

Safety has been improved by the twin engine configuration, but if things do go wrong do not lose time by searching for the ejection seat! The only solution is to unfasten your harness (seat harness not 'chute harness......(it has been done – Ed)), to jettison the canopy and bailing out. In fact this procedure requires some practice to be performed with any efficiency for you must dive under the wing if you are in the front seat or crawl on the wing if you are in the rear seat. Quite an interesting experience, particularly if the aircraft is out of control!

For the landing you initially maintain 17,000rpm to prevent flameout. You can sustain 0.75 mach (yes, a jet, remember!) and then 375kts IAS below 15,000 feet for a rapid descent. During the dive the non powered ailerons firm up (as previously mentioned) but all the other controls remain smooth and precise. Once in the circuit, your downwind speed will be 130 knots with the gear down and at 120 kts with full flaps you will certainly be the fastest man in the pattern at many airfields. So take care when operating amongst other types of aircraft. If for

instance you are number two behind a Rallye Club flying at 70 knots you are flying at approximately twice its speed!

The final approach is generally made at 110 knots and the threshold crossed at 90-95 knots. You must be cautious and look for flare as the elevators remain sensitive at such a low speed. The Magister encounters some ground effect with its very short undercart and when just above the ground.

As a jet the Magister does not like grass very much, but it is possible to operate the type from this surface as long as it is dry. During the rainy days it is best to hangar fly your Magister as this three ton machine will dig some holes in the touch down area, damage the undercart where it sinks into the ground and suck up mud into the air intakes. Stick to concrete!

During the restoration work, if any, you must inspect the wing spar and its attachment very closely because this is an aircraft that has been in service over thirty years and the type has generally been flown intensively for school and aerobatics training. Some Magisters are

Seen here in Finnish Air Force service as serial FM27 at Helsinki on 23rd November 1973, this aircraft is now registered in the United States as N604DM to the Which way is up? company of Miami, Florida. (Hannu Valtonen)

Fouga Fever!

still airworthy but not cleared for aerobatics where wing attachment inspection revealed some damaged bolts.

To sum up the Magister is a valuable fun aircraft to operate as a warbird. The twin-engine and two-seat configuration is a good combination. An operating budget should not reach unreasonable levels and once the French government has phased all Magisters out of active military service I shall enjoy flying mine to the limit!

WARBIRDS
W O R L D W I D E
JETS

Jim Porter's ex French Fouga CM170 serial 354 registration N302FM in Patrouille de France colours (**via Adrian Balch**). *The rear cockpit canopy is blanked out to allow adequate cooling of avionics.*

This shot of CM170 number 31 shows to advantage the dual tandem cockpits and the unique (in the jet world) periscope system. Radios and Nav gear is clearly visible through the rear cockpit section. (**J.C. Lu tringer**).

Roland Fraissinet in the Verdon-engined Mystere IVA which was overhauled by SOGERMA in Bordeaux after it was retired from active service in October 1982. It is hoped this aircraft will shortly be joined by a Mirage IIIC.

Dassault Mystere IV

The Mystere IVA was first flown on September 28th 1952, and 325 were ordered for the French *Armee de L'Air*. It was operational with the French Air Force for almost thirty years. The aircraft I fly is (serial number 315) powered by a single 7,710lb.s.t. Hispano Suiza Verdon engine, more powerful than the Rolls-Royce Tay version. It last served with the *8ieme Escadre de Chasse* in Cazaux.

The Mystere was entrusted to me by the French Ministry of Defence in October 1982 with the objective of keeping it airworthy as long as possible to display it as airshows within the *Association Les Ailes Francaises de la Chasse* of which I am President, and I expect similarly to take over, sooner or later, the last of the Mirage IIIC aircraft.

When 315 was delivered to my Association it was accompanied by a large spares holding including major components and spare engines. It was, nethertheless due for a major overhaul of the airframe and systems. This was undertaken by SOGERMA in Bordeaux, a major state owned workshop specialising in jet fighter overhaul. We also completely renewed the instrumentation – replacing several instruments with more modern

One type that is often overlooked on the warbird jet front is the Mystere IV. **Roland Fraissinet** takes a brief look at the aircraft he operates in France

Mirage equipment, including the avionics. The aircraft is now certified IFR by civilian standards and is flown as such.

Maximum permissible airspeed is 625 knots which is easily achieved in level flight. Maximum Mach is 1.2 which is more difficult to attain, although Mach 1 can be exceeded at full power in a shallow dive with no adverse behaviour from the aircraft. Normal approach speed is 180 knots and landing speed 150 knots; there is no drag chute and a minimum runway length of 7,000 feet is required to operate the Mystere safely. Ejection seat is a Martin Baker YAM 4 which permits ejection on take off above 90 knots.

The Mystere IV is more difficult to fly than a modern fighter such as the Mirage F.1 or Mirage 2000, although the early Mirage III, B, E and R were more tricky! Landing speed and stall speed are higher than the Mirage 2000, stall characteristics are poor, braking effect is equally poor and manoeuvrability very much inferior to a Mirage F.1 and even more the Mirage 2000. Roughly speaking in aerobatics or combat you cannot safely pull more than 2Gs at 200 knots, 3Gs at 300 knots and it is only above 400 knots that you can more or less pull anything (4G to 7G) without concern. Beyond these

35

figures, if you go too far you may experience a severe pitch-up which will cause loss of control and possibly structural damage in the most adverse circumstances. When, as I have done repeatedley these last few years – you step out of a Spitfire after performing a display and fly the Mystere, you must keep this in mind; if you treat the Mystere the same as the Spitfire you could easily break your neck!

Nevertheless it is a delightful aircraft to fly on aerobatics with lovely ailerons, comparable with those of the Gnat, and remarkably fast. It is displayed within our association by three pilots including myself. The two others are Lieutenant Chalande, currently a fighter pilot in the French Air Force, and Commandant Denis Legrand, test pilot. WW Roland Fraissinet.

MiG Alley Latest

Activities have been boosted lately at both MiG centres in the United States, with the import of large numbers of fresh MiG jets of varying mark. At **Reno** the first of 24 MiG-21s have arrived, probably from **Poland** but at this stage it is uncertain whether they are for Government contract work, warbird use or a mixture of both. In any event the first aircraft were here in September. At **Chino** several MiG–17s and MiG–19s have been showing up including two aircraft from **China**. Further supplies of MiG–15s have been imported by Warren Sessler, and more are expected. Most of the warbird operators at Chino now have a MiG of one sort or another and several are being rebuilt; the latest Chino product is a MiG–19 rolled out of Bruce Goessling's operation. No doubt the aircraft will be in big demand for film, advertising and promotional work (for Vodka advertising for example?).

Two seat MiG–15UTI's are a rarity with this example from Poland (one of four from there so far – **Robb Satterfield photo**) *and* **Lower (Thierry Thomassin)** *this Chino based MiG–15UTI appears to be from China if the style of markings is anything to go by. It has recently been registered to Warren Sessler as N7013N.*

JETS

Top and Centre (Jim Cawiezell) *MiG–15s in colourful Iraqi Air Force markings and insignia bask in the sun at Reno. Gone are the days when the baddies are poorly disguised Sabres!* **Lower (Thierry Thomassin)** *Planes of Fame at Chino have an ex Polish MiG–17 in the shape of IC9617.*

Sensational Sabre (Continued from Page 18)

North American F-86s and Canadair CL-13s on the United States Register as at 1st October 1988

Model	Serial	Owner
Canadair CL-13B		
N86CD	504	Corporate Jets Incs., Scottsdale, Arizona.
Canadair Sabre 6		
N106JB	23684	John MacGuire, Ft. Hancock, Texas.
N38301	1461	Tracor Flight Systems Inc. Santa Ana, California.
N3831B	1468	Tracor Flight Systems Inc.
N3841V	1459	Flight Systems Inc., Newport Beach, California.
N3842H	1472	Tracor Flight Systems Inc.
N3842J	1480	Tracor Flight Systems Inc.
N3844E	1482	Tracor Flight Systems Inc.
N38453	1487	Tracor Flight Systems Inc.
N3846J	1489	Tracor Flight Systems Inc.
N4688J	999	Sale Reported, Redstone Arsenal, Alabama.
N46882	1012	Sale Reported, Redstone Arsenal, Alabama.
N4689H	1083	Southern California Aviation Inc. Corona Del Mar, California.
N4689N	1128	Sale Reported, Redstone Arsenal, Alabama.
N50CJ	381	Corporate Jets Inc. Scottsdale, Arizona.
N74180	886	Sale Reported, Newport Beach, California.
N80FS	1675	Tracor Flight Systems Inc.
N82FS	1600	Tracor Flight Systems Inc.
N8686F	1153	Boeing Equipment Holding Co., Seattle, Washington.
N87FS	1491	Tracor Flight Systems Inc.
N89FS	1710	Tracor Flight Systems Inc.
N93FS	1137	Tracor Flight Systems Inc.
N96125	1058	Sale Reported
F-86 Mk 5		
N72492	1105	Sale Reported
N74170	1110	Sale Reported
N86FS	1157	Sale Reported
N86JR	1120	Combat Jets Flying Museum, Houston, Texas.
N8687D	1104	Combat Jets Flying Museum, Houston, Texas.
N91FS	23231	Tracor Flight Systems Inc.
N92FS	1075	Tracor Flight Systems Inc.
N98230	980	Sale Reported
N98250	1049	Sale Reported
N98279	1113	Sale Reported

Colour Captions Opposite: Thierry Thomassin *captured the* Combat Jet's *Canadair Sabre N8687D before it's spectacular Korean warpaint was applied at Mojave in November 1987. Even naked the Sabre is a classic beauty.* **Lower:** *Some 14 years earlier* **Bill Larkings** *shot N8686D at Reno with Bob Hoover at the controls. this aircraft is a CL13 Mk. 5, ex CF-BKG, RCAF 23285. It was sold to* Flight Systems Inc. *as N92FS some years later.* **Top (Combat Jets Flying Museum)** *N8687D dressed as The Huff in company with the Museum's MiG–15.*

39

Sensational Sabre

North American F-86

N306X	1096	Sale Reported
N5591N	985	Sale Reported, Orlando, Florida.
N74062	53-1040	AMCEP Inc. Tucson, Arizona.
N178	48-178	Ben W. Hall, Seattle, Washington.
N57964	49-1324	Ben Hall, Seattle, Washington.
N57965	47-606	Sale Reported
N25143	52-5143	Lesley L. Crowder, Sunland, California.
N51RS	51-13417	Mid-Atlantic Air Museum, Middletown, Penna.
N57963	52-4608	Robert D. Scott, San Martin, California.
N57966	51-2884	Ben W. Hall, Seattle, Washington.
N86F	52-5139A	Exotics Leasing Corporation, Santa Barbara, California.
N7006G	SA.111	Rick Sharpe, Rosharon, Texas.
N7006J	SA.119	Rick Sharpe, Rosharon, Texas.
N86RJ	51-6071	Robert Alan Kemp, Reno, Nevada.

North American FJ-4B

N400FS	143575	Tracor Flight Systems Inc. Santa Ana, California.

GNATS!

The Folland and Hindustan Aeronautics Gnat Aircraft are proving to be popular as a small Warbird jet. Several ex Indian Air Force *Adjeets* are in store at Chino, California, awaiting rebuild – amongst them are *Adjeets* (equivalent of Gnat F.1s) IE276, IE296, IE1076, IE1214 and IE1222. Large numbers of Royal Air Force two seat tandem Gnat trainers are also coming up for disposal. Of those already sold by the Ministry of Defence several have found their way to North America including this example being rebuilt by Carl Scholl at *Aero Traders* at Chino, California. As the Gnat scene develops we will be reporting on it in future issues of **WARBIRDS WORLDWIDE.**

From **Mick Allen** *comes this shot of the recently painted Gnat G-BOXP owned by Arnold Glass* **Top** *whilst an anonymous ex RAF Gnat, stripped down for rebuild by* Aero Traders *at Chino was captured by Warbirds photographer* **Thierry Thomassin.**

40

Once Bitten!

The finished Vampire with yours truly at the controls in partnership with Robb Satterfield, the Warbirds Worldwide Chief Pilot.

Have you ever been bitten by a *Vampire?* I heard tell it was a lethal occurrence at best, so when I heard that a *Vampire* was lurking around a southern Texas airport, I just had to find out for myself! And yes, it is lethal. Lethal to your sanity, your love life and most of all, your cheque book!

It was the spring of 1986 when a chance meeting brought me into contact with the owner of a de Havilland Mark 35 Vampire. He wanted to sell and I, oblivious to the world of reality wanted to buy, After all, I had been looking for a warbird for some time but something always stood in my way (usually money!). I had dreamed of owning a jet, for I felt that the jet warbird scene was about to happen and I wanted to be in the midst of it when it did. A wild dream, I assured myself, for repeated forays through *Trade-A-Plane* and the like only reinforced my suspicions that my dreams were on an unreachable financial level. And seeing as I rarely had dreams of making lots of money, I knew I was doomed to a life of jet dreams.

Somehow we were able to consummate the deal in only 8 or 9 months, and in January 1987 I became the proud owner of November 11926. Honest advice by an acquaintance, now a good friend, Ed Stead, helped me over-rule the fact that I had never even heard the engine run and I boldly told my new landlord that I would have the beast out of there before summer. It is funny how one switches from abject suspicion to blatant confidence with a simple change of ownership!

As most of you who have already restored aircraft know, time has a funny way of passing by without much apparent accomplishment. I also believe the telephone company is indirectly involved in first time projects such as this, for my

Charles Parnall tells of his experiences rebuilding a de Havilland T.35 Vampire in Texas, U.S.A.

phone bill began to look like a small version of our national debt. Fortunately, there are people like Ed Stead to field the many, many questions that crop up in the novice's mind. I was also very fortunate in coming in contact with John Epperson, who had spent many hours on this very Vampire when it first came to Texas some 16 years earlier. Both these men, as well as a very understanding girlfriend who was not afraid to get her hands dirty, were crucial to my early success.

Our first engine start attempt was slated for May 17, 1987. All the parts chasing and running around in circles; all the testing, the timing, the broken skin and frustrated weekends; all these things were instantly thrust into the background as the engine began to wind up. The igniters cracked like a coachman's whip and, after 15 or 20 seconds that seemed like minutes, the unmistakable sound of a *Goblin* engine spooling up under its own power shattered the quiet southern Texas air. It ran! Of course, I knew it would all along – it's just nice to be able to say 'I told you so' rather than . . .! I was so "high" the next week that I was on 100% oxygen most of the time!

But like most restorations, there are 'lows' to accompnay some of the 'highs'. Mine was no exception for the very next weekend saw me and my girlfriend deluged with stick hydraulic fluid – the result of a ruptured hydraulic tank positioned strategically behind our heads! This particular problem caused several things to happen: the worst was a 3 month wait for a replacement tank

while the best was discovering the friendship of Sandy Topen and the *Vintage Aircraft Team* at Cranfield, England. My girlfriend? She took it all in good spirits and became a 'redhead' for a while.

As you might have guessed by now, I had to extend my lease on the hangar. Summer turned to autumn and I was still a long way off completing the project. September was a red letter day for the United States for that was the month we were blessed by the fine folks from the *Vintage Aircraft Team.* Of course I saw right through Monsigneur Topen's phony accent and pristine appearance and was able to extract some actual hands-on work from the man! (In spite of what you may have heard, Sandy Topen does get his hands dirty. Not on airplanes, mind, but nevertheless, he does get them dirty!) Actually, Sandy and his assistant, Gary Cook, were a great help and, along with my two friends and helpers, Bob Wells and Jim Clemons, we were able to accomplish many of the checks and inspections I was unable to do on my own. Real progress was showing – especially after we took Gary to a 'gentleman's club'! (Not to mention the female 'jogger' that made working evenings a pleasure!)

When things finally settled back to normal following the visit from across the pond, we began our taxi testing and also began attacking the wooden fuselage that was showing some signs of neglect. This brought out a few more problems and so the next 3 months dragged on without incident until December, when Sandy Topen and Peter Hoare managed to once again slip by the U.S. customs agents and visit the project. This time I was able to see the great Scot in action – doing paperwork! The 'odd couple' departed, giving the Vampire an English-Scots

blessing and it was now time to get serious about having the jet licensed. As this is best left to a professional, I asked Rick Sharpe of *Warbirds Unlimited* of Texas to take over. Rick is one of the U.S.A.'s leading jet warbird preparation experts, having handled Vampires, Venoms, Hispano Saetas, Fouga Magisters and an F–86 Sabre, He also had a Letter of Authorization on the Vampire and could check me out after he finished the aircraft. We planned to fly the Vampire away from its home of 17 years or so sometime after the first of the new year.

We had done our homework well! The day finally arrived when the weather was perfect, the aircraft was ready, and the pilots . . . well, the pilots were late due to a cancelled flight by an uncaring airline. So, instead of a perfect day, we ended up with an acceptable day. Isn't that how most plans end up?

Not having a proper radio (other than a backup handheld), we decided to have another friend, Ken Camp, take off in his Beech Baron and orbit while we did some last minute checks and then pushed the throttle to its forward stop and waited through the first take-off in too many years. I cannot explain the feelings we experienced during this first take-off, but they are hard to beat – especially when everything worked as it should! We formated on Ken's wing and landed at New Braunfels airport for fuel prior to heading over to Rick's hangar in Houston, Texas. Surprisingly, we were not stuck to the seat, and were able to leap out of the aircraft and brag on how cool we were during that wonderful first flight! Time and success works wonders.

The rest of the journey was uneventful and the Vampire flew beautifully. Control harmony was obvious and all the systems operated correctly. It was a perfect blend of relief and pride and it made all those countless hours worthwhile. It was a great day!

Reluctantly, I returned to San Antonio for what my girlfriend hoped would be a more sane schedule while Rick performed the FAA approved flight test program on the Vampire. Unfortunately that was not to be as I was now forced to repent for my laziness after leaving the military by having to update my naked private pilot's license with a least an instrument and commercial endorsement. Ground schools and more flying managed to destroy the 'dating dollars' once again and then it was time for me to start my check-out on the Vampire.

Now for those of you who aren't really into the finer points of owning and flying a jet, let me state right now that owning a jet is the easiest way I know of becoming a millionaire – you simply start with 2 million! At 300 – 350 *gallons* per hour, you don't want to be making too many mistakes. Retakes are very expensive! It wasn't long before the cash reserves ran dry and so what else was there but the *American Express*. Don't fly a jet without it. Fly now, pay later really had an impact on me when 'later' first came. It was more like 'fly now, pay forever'! I still cannot believe how fast this jet can convert a month's salary into a few minutes memory; It is a true 'jet-a-holic'.

During this exciting phase, we encountered but one problem in a bad nose wheel shimmy, which necessitated changing the unit with a rebuilt one that came with the aircraft. So now it was time to make it look like a new kid on the block. Finding a paint scheme that compliments the bulbous nose of the two-seat Vampire is not easy. Finding an attractive scheme that was used in combat was almost impossible, were it not for a bit of help from the RAF Museum and a tip from Richard Kelwood in Oxfordshire, England. The answer lay in the scheme used by the Rhodesian Air

Force and carried on by the Air Force of Zimbabwe. A friend in Zimbabwe let me borrow the orginal blueprint of the layout while another friend in South Africa sent me detailed photographs of logos and markings. We used poetic license with the colours and ended up with a fairly accurate copy of the glossy camouflage scheme. I think you will agree that it makes this Vampire rather unique and rather attractive – if I do say so myself. I also wish to point out that one most remarkable thing about this entire project is the willingness of others to lend a hand when asked – irregardless of their background. It seems that those interested in aviation (of any era) are more than willing to help another aircraft return to the skies for which it was made. There is something wonderful about the 'thing' that trancends most man-made boundaries. I am a better person for having experienced it.

I know you are expecting me to finish with an 'all's well that ends well' type of finish. Unfortunately, that is not quite accurate, for during an air show at Houston Gulf airport, we developed engine problems. Serious problems. An engine change was required, but again good fortune smiled on my worthless self when it turned out that a spare engine we had was fresh from at least a hot section overhaul, and so it was back to Rick Sharpe's hangar with my friend, ex USAF engine tech. Mackey Clemons, for a 6 day crash course of Vampire engine changing. We timed it perfectly as I made it back to San Antonio on Wednesday, October 5th so that I could put off my creditors Thursday morning, gather up my girlfriend, and jet to the Confederate Air Force Airsho 88 in Harlingen. I had been looking forward to participating in that great warbird event and was not disappointed. It was a great season finale to a wonderful year with the Vampire.

As I reflect on the past 20 months, more or less, I count myself amongst the fortunate few. I was able to realize a dream – a dream I never thought would become reality. I was fortunate in being able to find such a project and get it airworthy without any major expenditures (other than fuel), and I am fortunate in being able to count new friends in several different countries around the world as a result of this project. I believe that the jet warbird movement is just now

coming into its own, with not only Vampires and Venoms and and T–33's, but MiG 15's, –17's and maybe –21's, Hawker Hunters in single and two seat versions, F–86 Sabres, Panthers, Saetas in a wide variety of trims, Fouga Magisteres, A–4 Skyhawks, F–5's, T–38's, and even a CF–104. And more may be standing in the wings. It is exciting for all of us because now we can truly say that we are preserving the entire spectrum of flight, from its beginning to the modern military hardware. No longer do airshows have to have a gap in their program between World War II and the present. Now they can show it all. So spread the word: 'the jets are coming'. And the time isn't far off when you will see an all-jet airshow or at least an all-jet feature attraction. The interest is out there and we are available. Support your local jets!!

T-Birds Three

The Lockheed T–33s and TV–2s plus the Canadair Silver have spearheaded the jet warbird movement for many years. The aircraft are still as popular as ever and here we take an illustrated look at three of the aircraft currently being operated in the United States.

Douglas Clark's Canadair Silver Star Mk 3 currently with George Baker's American Aero Services at Daytona Beach in Florida has recently been painted in tunderbirds markings after rebuild at that facility (**Jackson Flinn**).

Thierry Thomassin *caught the former Leroy penhall Lockheed TV2 N6633D outside in the sun at Chino in September 1988* (**Top and Lower (Mike Beatley)** *dazzling white with a blue trim and red cheatlines is Canadair Silver Star No. 375 alias N33HW owned by Jet I Incorporated of Alexanderia, Virginia, at the same location.*

43

MiG-21 Profile

John Wilmslow looks at the latest new warbird import to the United States, the MiG-21 Fishbed.

The MiG-21 flew for the first time in 1955, making its public debut in the Soviet Union in June the following year. It was not a coincidence that this appearance occurred almost three years after cessation of hostilities in Korea. For the MiG-21, NATO code-name Fishbed, was the answer to the shortcomings of the MiG-15 and early marks of 17. It is a well documented fact that the MiG-15 had been outclassed by the classic F-86 Sabre; the latter's superior transonic handling had sent many MiG-15 drivers spinning to their deaths.

The design concept behind the MiG-21 demanded effective firepower based on an exceptional climb rate to deal with intruding high-altitude bombers. The Soviet designers had also built into the MiG-21 the ability to fight whatever their compatriots had up their sleeve as successors to the Sabre, Hunter and their French equivalents.

The MiG-17 – a less than harsh refinement of the Mig-15 was entering service at the close of the Korean war and the MiG-19, a twin engined Mach 1.4 fighter prototype was just commencing trials. The MiG-15 family had, so far, all been

Chinese built Xian F7 – the equivalent of an early Soviet MiG–21 Fishbed C at Peking in China (**Top by Gerry Manning**). *Note the pitot tube mounted underneath the nose, the forward tilting canopy and the canon.* **Above (Jim Cawiezell)** *Seemingly Poland is the source of this early MiG–21 variant seen in the hangar at Reno.*

comparatively lightweight fighters and though the pressure was on the Mikoyan design house to produce a heavier fighter to carry much larger bomber-destroying missiles a quirk of fate – a Sidewinder missile, lodged in the rear fuselage of a MiG-17 fell into Communist hands – and this, coupled with the brief that the new model should be cost effective to produce (ie a lot of aircraft at low unit cost) plus the fact that smaller aircraft present much less of a target probably had enough bearing to give the MiG-21 the edge over other aircraft in the running as replacements for the earlier MiGs. In any event the MiG-21 was to become the mainstay of the Soviet fighting powers.

It was many years before western observers were able to see the MiG-21 and longer before they were allowed access to the cockpit. 1963 saw Finland take delivery of MiG-21-F-12s but the Soviets demanded a high level of security at Fishbed airfields in an attempt to foil western intelligence from gaining hard facts on the type.

However, this was to change in 1966 when a defecting Iraqi pilot flew his aircraft to Israel, with the result that U.S. specialists were allowed to examine the aircraft and its avionics and systems. A year later, during the six day war the United States were given a present when three Algerian MiG-21s landed at El Arish, unaware that the airfield had been captured by Israeli Forces.

It is understood that at least three of these aircraft were disassembled, loaded aboard USAF aircraft and flown to the USA for examination and evaluation.

Like most other fighters the MiG-21 evolved from the early development model Fishbed A and B into the first mass produced '21 variant the Fishbed C. After only a short time in service the MiG-21's Tumansky RD11 powerplant, initially rated at just 8600lb (11,240lb with afterburner) was uprated and the aircraft re-designated MiG-21F, though the NATO designation remained unchanged. For the later variants delivered to the Soviet Air Force were designated MiG-21PF, the letter P meaning interceptor. The latter was dubbed Fishbed D by NATO. This D introduced a larger air intake and the pitot static tube was removed from the lower section of the nose to the top section. Revised cockpit canopy coupled with the deletion of attitude vanes were two basic recognition features. Fuselage cannon fairings were removed and forward speed brakes installed. Larger mainwheels were fitted to a much sturdier undercart.

The parachute braking system was the next for attention. The Fishbed C and D models had its chute housed in a compartment alongside the ventral fin. This system was improved by utilising a bullet shaped fairing at the base of the fin. The fin was eventually extended, eliminating the root fillet. This change was incorporated to improve supersonic handling and this, complete with other refinements lead to the Fishbed D and E variants, both of which saw action in North Vietnam. The next progression, the Fishbed F utilised a simpler ejection

seat system – the initial Fishbed ejector seats utilised the cockpit canopy to protect the escaping pilot from blast. Subsequently the system was to prove unsatisfactory and the new canopy on the F hinged to the right instead of tilting forwards. It was this type of Fishbed that the Indian Air Force manufactured with the label type 77, and Czechoslovakia developed into the MiG-21SPS. Several other versions evolved but we have covered the main types here.

Potentially more attractive to warbird operators will be the two-seat operational trainer version of the series, the MiG-21UTI. NATO allocated code name Mongol to this fighter. Initially, the Mongol A was introduced and this appeared to be almost a field modification, with a second seat inserted behind the normal cockpit position. The two seat version was progressively developed into the Mongol B version incorporating some of the refinements of the later model single seat Fishbeds. One very clever feature of all later model MiG-21s is that the ejection seat sequence cannot be initiated whilst the hood is open, thus ruling out any accidents whilst being serviced on the ground.

It has to be said that the MiG-21 will

probably be a very difficult type of aircraft to operate. The Soviet versions are powered by a Tumansky RD-11 dash 300 twin spool turbojet, which is apparently only good for less than 300 hours between overhaul, compared to say 700 hours on an Avon. All fuel is stored in the fuselage, mainly due to the thin wing. Most western fighters have fully duplicated hydraulics systems; the MiG-21 has only a single system. If the single system fails to provide enough pressure an electric driven pump takes over, but if the aircraft suffers a dual failure then the pilot is in trouble. No doubt ingenuity will come to the fore when rebuilding these aircraft for civilian use. Endurance is severely limited with typical sortie endurance (without wing tanks) of little over 30 minutes, similar to a Lightning. The MiG-21 is very lightweight in every sense though it suffers from a shortage of power.

Many western defence experts view the MiG-21 as a rather pathetic machine with inadequate armament and poor airfield performance. This, coupled with poor power and potentially expensive frequent engine changes makes the MiG-21 an expensive proposition. WW John Wilmslow.

DATA: MiG-21

Name: MiG-21 (NATO code Fishbed – two seat trainer MiG-21 UTI Mongol.
Powerplant: One Tumansky RD11 powerplant rated at 10,000lb.s.t. dry and 12,500lb with reheat.
Dimensions: (MiG-21F) Span 25 ft. Height 14 ft 6 ins. Length: 47ft. Wing area: 250 Sq ft.
Performance: Max speed clean 1320 mph at 36,000 ft. With drop tanks and two Atoll missiles: 990 mph. Range: 1260 miles with one 130 gallon drop tank.

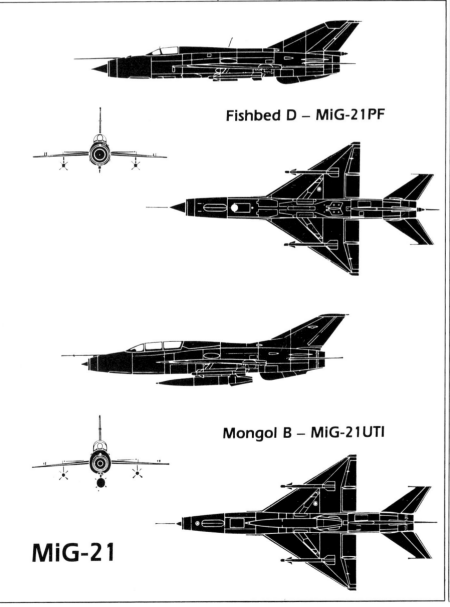

Fishbed D – MiG-21PF

Mongol B – MiG-21UTI

MiG-21

Last of the Lightning Pilots (Continued from Page 20)

realise there is still a long way to go. Electronic Counter Measures (ECM) Night Practice Intercepts (PIs), air-to-air refuelling by day and by night and air-to-air gunnery. Missile practice camps and 'Saturn' PIs; attacks from 250 feet to 55,000 feet, any height, heading or speed.

I often reflected after several sorties that I had just flown one of the world's greatest fighters. Admittedly it had no amazing radar and no radar missiles but on a clear day it's still a classic fighter, and now a real warbird. Hopefully, it won't be long before we see a Lightning in the air again.

I often wondered, in 1988, as I thought the Lightning was so good, what it was like to fly it in 1958 – and try to compare it then to now, the F–16s of today. Operators of Lightning on the civilian registers are going to have their own small problems. Admittedly they won't be related to the weapons or radar systems as these can be deleted. Obviously operating a Lightning won't be cheap, but neither is rebuilding a Lancaster from scratch, so it can be done.

One of the critical factors of operating a Lightning in civil hands will undoubtedly be the engineering set-up. Specialist tools will almost certainly be needed for engine changes, removal of the jet pipes and any major work on the aircraft's antiquated electrical system. Before any safety conscious pilot would ever climb into a Lightning, particularly with its poor safety record, the ejector seats will have to be in tip-top condition, undergoing regular servicing by qualified Martin-Baker personnel. This, I believe could cost up to £25,000 per seat. Lightning mainwheel tyres fit no other aircraft, and even have to be specially built for each aircraft, though I gather sufficient supplies remain in stock. Almost unique to the Lightning (although the Canberra PR.9 and the Saab Drakens operating in Denmark also use it) is the highly volatile AVPIN starter fluid. For this you would need an explosives licence to house. Again, only a small quantity of this fluid is manufactured per month and the figures around £40 per gallon have been quoted. Six

gallons are used for two starts of the engines. Most important of all would be to remain current on the aircraft ie flying at least 20 to 30 hours per summer season if any sort of safe display was to be performed. However, with a little willpower and enough determination I am sure these problems can be overcome. I feel that realistically the two seat variant of the aircraft will be the most economical to fly. Other major factors affecting a decision as to whether a flying licence could be granted for the Lightning would be the length of runway it was to be operated from. 6,000 feet will be the absolute minimum you could use to operate the aircraft safely. Whether or not I would like to fly a civilian Lightning remains another story, but should one appear at an airshow, I'd be the first to go and see it! **WW Ian Black**

Ian Black is the author of LIGHTNING published by Airlife and it is available at £13.95 Casebound or £8.95 Paperback from Airlife Publishing Limited, 7 St. John's Hill, Shrewsbury, Shropshire SY1 1JE.

JETS